When Christians Disagree
Series Editor: Oliver R. Barclay

The Role of Women
Editor: Shirley Lees

Other titles in this series

Pacifism and War
Editor: Oliver R. Barclay

Creation and Evolution
Editor: Derek Burke

In preparation

Charismatic Gifts
Politics

The Role of Women

Editor: Shirley Lees

WHEN CHRISTIANS DISAGREE

Joyce Baldwin
Elizabeth Catherwood
David Field
Michael Griffiths
Valerie Griffiths
James B. Hurley
Daphne Key
I. Howard Marshall

Inter-Varsity Press

INTER-VARSITY PRESS
38 De Montfort Street, Leicester LE1 7GP, England

First published 1984
Reprinted 1985, 1987

British Library Cataloguing in Publication Data
The role of women.—(When Christians disagree)
1. Women—Social conditions   2. Women in
Christianity
I. Lees, Shirley   II. Baldwin, Joyce
III. Series
261.8'3442   HQ1394

ISBN 0–85110–721–4

Set in Linotron Sabon
Phototypeset in Great Britain by
Input Typesetting Ltd, London SW19 8DR
Printed in Great Britain
at the University Press, Oxford

*Inter-Varsity Press is the publishing division of the Universities
and Colleges Christian Fellowship (formerly the Inter-Varsity
Fellowship), a student movement linking Christian Unions in
universities and colleges throughout the United Kingdom and
the Republic of Ireland, and a member movement of the
International Fellowship of Evangelical Students. For
information about local and national activities write to UCCF,
38 De Montfort Street, Leicester LE1 7GP.*

When Christians Disagree

Introducing the series

There are many subjects on which the teaching of the Bible is quite clear. There is a substantial core of Christian theology and ethics that we can confidently proclaim as 'biblical teaching', and those rejecting as well as those accepting the authority of that teaching will agree that such a core exists.

As we try to work out the application of biblical teaching in detail, however, we find areas in which there is no such clear consensus. Christians who are trying equally to be obedient to the teaching of Christ and his carefully instructed apostles come to different conclusions about such subjects as baptism and church government. Some of their differences have been resolved after debate. In Protestant circles, for instance, few would now wish, as some once did, to excommunicate people for advocating birth control. Further discussion has brought substantial agreement. Some questions, however, are not so easily resolved at present; and there is a need for healthy discussion among Christians so that we may arrive, if possible, at an agreed view. If that is not possible, then all of us need to re-examine our view in the light of Scripture and to exchange views, so that we may ensure that our position is not the product of wishful thinking, but is really faithful to the Bible. All of us are influenced in our thinking by

5

our traditions, our education and the general climate of thought of our age. These forces tend to mould our ideas more than we realize, and to make us conform to the fashion of our time, or the traditions in which we were brought up, rather than to revealed truth.

This series of books under the title of *When Christians Disagree* attempts to tackle some of these current debates. Each book has the same fundamental structure. A series of starting 'theses', or a statement of a position (usually excluding the more extreme views on either side), has been sent to the writers. They have been asked to agree or disagree with the 'theses' and to set out a Christian position as they see it. They then have the opportunity to respond to one or more of the other articles written from a different point of view from their own. A short closing summary attempts to clarify the main issues in debate.

All the contributors seek to be ruled by Scripture. Since they do not agree between themselves, the crucial issue is whether one view or another is more consistent with the teaching of the Bible. Some of the problems arise out of the impact upon us of new cultural patterns. These new patterns may or may not be healthy, and that has to be judged by the application of biblical truth which is always health-giving – the good and acceptable and perfect will of God. We are not arguing whether it is easier to believe or do one thing or another in today's world. We are not even asking whether a Christian position seems stupid to the cultured man of today. We are asking whether there are revealed principles that give us at least some guidelines, and perhaps even a clear answer to our problems.

The Bible is authoritative in more than one way: in some areas explicit teaching is given; in other areas the question is left open in such a way that we know there is no universal 'right' answer. Worship provides an example. There are some broad principles; but the Bible seems authoritatively to allow, and perhaps implicitly to encourage, variety in the details of the style and ordering of worship. In such cases we will solve the problem in our own age and culture in obedience to the more basic explicit teachings that we have.

Introducing the series

In the areas that this series explores there are some things laid down clearly in Scripture and some that are not. There is, for instance, no biblical instruction as to whether husband or wife should dig the garden; there are no explicit limits drawn to the coercive powers of the state, nor any delineation of the nature of the world before the fall – except that it was very good.

The arguments, therefore, concern first of all whether the Bible does or does not settle certain questions and, secondly, how far we can go in confident application of those biblical truths that we are given. The demarcation line between these here is important. If we can agree what is clearly taught then all else is in a secondary category, where we know that human opinion is fallible. Some of our discussion is above the line and is therefore most important. Some falls below it and cannot be as vital, even if in practical terms we have to adopt a policy.

OLIVER R. BARCLAY

Contents

9

Part 2

Introduction:
Women, equal but different

Equality and freedom are popular concepts in today's world, not least among those who are campaigning on behalf of women. As Christians of the twentieth century we would agree whole-heartedly that all men and women are created equal in God's sight. But although Christianity has been to the forefront in the emancipation of women, not all Christians are agreed on how freedom and equality work out in practice, either in male/female relationships or in the church.

Is marriage a partnership of equals, differing only biologically, or is it a relationship between two equal but very different people, with the headship vested in the man? What does 'headship' mean, anyway? Does Scripture teach the silence of women in the church, or encourage women to use their God-given gifts in ministry in the church in other than purely 'feminine' roles? What does it *really* say?

The Women's Liberation movement is causing a considerable amount of rethinking of our understanding of Scripture, which is breaking into long-held traditional interpretations. Some have felt threatened by this and have withdrawn into more deeply entrenched positions. Others have seen the possibility of change but are in danger of throwing the baby out with the bathwater. Of course we cannot allow secular thinking to shape our interpretation of Scripture, but we can be thankful that it challenges us to submit with fresh openness to the Word of God.

That is the aim of all the contributors to this book. They have been asked to write because they are known to be men and women who are committed to a belief in the authority of Scripture and are eager to learn from it and direct their living and thinking by it. However, whether we like it or not, God has allowed his people the freedom over the centuries to have varying interpretations of those parts of Scripture which do not directly affect our faith in the perfect and finished work of Christ. If that were not so, we could be in the obviously extremely dangerous position (albeit unconsciously) of a most ardent and devout missionary friend who said to my husband many years ago: 'But, doctor, if an interpretation of Scripture is correct, it is no longer an interpretation, but Scripture.'

Such a view unconsciously makes the mind of man as infallible as God's Word. It leaves no room for a loving tolerance of those Christians who hold different views. Further, it inhibits an examination of interpretations of Scripture held strongly over many years or even centuries, views which may turn out to be 'tradition' rather than Scripture.

This of course is a problem which faced the early church, not least on the subject of women. It was an age when women were regarded as inferior, not only by Greeks and Romans, but also by Jews, who were the custodians of God's Word. As several of our contributors have pointed out, Jewish men thanked God daily that they had not been born 'a Gentile, a woman or a slave'. Such a view was obviously affecting the church, and Paul refuted it in no uncertain terms. 'There is neither Jew nor Greek, there is neither slave nor free, there is neither male nor female; for you are all one in Christ Jesus' (Gal. 3:28).

Over the centuries equally committed Christians have given different interpretations of certain passages of Scripture referring to women. Today the same is true. We are very grateful to the contributors to this symposium, for being willing not only to grapple with some difficult ques-

Introduction: Women, equal but different

tions, but also to submit themselves to one another for criticism, while at the same time seeking to 'let the book that speaks for itself, speak' (as one contributor puts it).

SHIRLEY LEES

Starting-points

To provide an overview of the area of debate, the 'starting-points' which were sent to the contributors before they embarked on their papers are given below.

Equality of the sexes
The Bible teaches simultaneously the equality of the sexes (without egalitarianism) and the differences between, and complementarity of, the sexes (without superiority or inferiority).

1. *God created both men and women equally in his own image* (Gn. 1:26–27).

2. *All men and women, whether young or old, brilliant or handicapped, sophisticated or 'primitive', and whatever the colour of their skin, their culture, race or rank in society, are one and equal in the sight of God* (Gn. 1:27; Gal. 3:28; Acts 10:34).

3. *Woman was created as a helper for man and the sexes were created to be complementary and inter-dependent* (Gn. 2:18; 1 Cor. 11:11). What is the significance of 'helper'? Together they were commissioned to the task of filling the earth and subduing it (Gn. 1:28).

4. *The inter-dependence and equality of the sexes was distorted by the fall into male dominance and female subjection* (Gn. 3:16). Re-creation in Christ reverses that

14

distortion; but is the result a partnership of equals, or a hierarchy comprising man and his helper/counterpart? The principle of 'headship' remains (1 Cor. 11:3) within the context of Christian humility (Phil. 2:3); but what does it signify?

5. *Both men and women are equally called to be in relationship with God* (1 Pet. 3:7). Both are equally important and precious to him and both are capable of being used in his service. Jesus spent time teaching women and instructing them (*e.g.* Mary, the Syrophoenician woman and the woman at the well). Women were the first to witness the resurrection and to give witness to it.

6. *The Bible accepts that there are authority relationships between people, but that does not alter their equality as people.* Jesus himself always submitted to the Father (Jn. 6:38; 8:28–29) but remained equal with him (Jn. 5:18; 8:28–29). We are to submit, for the Lord's sake, to one another (Eph. 5:21) and to authorities (1 Pet. 2:13; Rom. 13:1). Children are to obey their parents (Eph. 6:1). Servants are to obey their masters (Eph. 6:5; 1 Pet. 2:13–18). Leaders are to be respected for their work (1 Thes. 5:12) and obeyed (Heb. 13:17), but all men and women are of equal importance to us as Christians (2 Cor. 6:16).

7. *There is stress in the New Testament on each Christian exercising his or her gifts.* All gifts are important to the health of the whole body (Eph. 4:12). None can be called unimportant. There is no stated differentiation as to whether these gifts are given to men or women (1 Cor. 12).

Women's role in society
1. *The Bible provides evidence of women as well as men taking an active part in society.* Deborah was a ruler of her country as well as a prophetess. Esther was a leading diplomat who was able to save her people from extinction. Lydia was a trader, Tabitha a well-known seamstress and social worker; and it is probable that Priscilla was a leading public figure.

2. Apart from these and similar illustrations, *there is*

no clear scriptural instruction or limitation set on the roles of either men or women in society generally.

3. Nevertheless, *women in the first century were regarded as inferior and had no legal rights.*

Women in marriage and the home

1. *All Christians are to submit to one another* (Eph. 5:21).

2. *Within that context, the relationship between men and women in the home is asymmetrical.* Wives are instructed to 'be subject to your husbands' (Eph. 5:22) and husbands are told to love their wives 'as Christ loved the church' (Eph. 5:25).

3. *Wives are also told, however, to submit to unbelieving husbands,* so that even those who do not believe may be won for Christ (1 Pet. 3:1).

4. *The husband is the head of the wife* (1 Cor. 11:3) *in a way that is parallel to that in which God is the Head of Christ.* Christ submitted totally to the Father (Jn. 4:34; 5:19, 30; 8:29, *etc.*), but remained totally equal with God (as above, 'Equality of the sexes', 6).

5. *Paul also relates this headship to creation* (1 Cor. 11:3, 11–12) and develops it as it applies to marriage, by comparing it to the relationship between Christ and the church. The distortion of the male/female relationship through the fall is restored in the partnership of the true marriage relationship, *i.e.* the self-giving love of the husband and the self-giving submission of the wife (Eph. 5:22–33).

6. *The ideal woman* (Pr. 31) *had considerable authority, managing her household (including servants) well.* But she was also a good business woman who did not neglect her children. Are there principles here for the arguments for or against 'working' mothers?

Women in the church

1. *On the basis of the exhortations to silence* (1 Cor. 14:34–35 and 1 Tim. 2:12) *many denominations have allowed women no part in public worship.* In contrast Miriam and Deborah were prophetesses, and women took

part in liturgical dance in Old Testament worship. In the New Testament, Anna was a prophetess (Lk. 2:36ff.) as were the unnamed daughters of Philip (Acts 21:9). There seems no indication that the gift of prophecy was not exercised by various Christians, irrespective of sex (1 Cor. 11:4ff.); and this fulfilled the prophecy that 'your sons and your daughters shall prophesy' (Joel 2:28).

2. *Paul says 'I permit no woman to teach or to have authority over men'* (1 Tim. 2:12). Is this a particular situation, or does the fact that he bases his argument on creation suggest a 'creation ordinance', giving an authority or leadership role to men? Was Huldah the prophetess 'teaching' as she explained the word of the Lord to the priest and the king's officials, when King Josiah could not understand 'the words of the book of the law'? (2 Ki. 22:11ff.).

3. *In all the passages about elders, there is no mention of women* (though some suggest 1 Timothy 5:1–2 indicates a parallel between elders and older women). There is equally no prohibition to women. There do appear to have been deacons who were women (1 Tim. 3:11), though some think this refers to deacons' wives.

4. *The Bible says very little about the role of single women (probably because there were so few), but widows occasionally seem to have played a particular role in church life* (1 Tim. 5:9–12, 'a widow who wants to become one of the special church workers', LB). Paul encouraged both men and women to remain single in order to be concerned about the 'Lord's affairs' (1 Cor. 7:32–35) and therefore presumably to take an active part in church life.

5. *Paul regarded a significant number of women as 'fellow-workers'* (Rom. 16 and Phil. 4:2–3). Women today play a prominent part in overseas missions. Why is it that God appears to have called more women than men, thus causing them to be in positions of leadership, at least temporarily?

6. *The New Testament has several names for leaders in congregations.* Some (evangelists, pastors, teachers, prophets) refer to God-given gifts of ministry to an indivi-

dual, exercised for the spiritual benefit of the members. Others have more reference to the ordering of church life (apostle, elder, overseer, bishop, deacon). It is hard to know how static or formal these offices were. Romans 16 speaks of individual women as deacons, fellow-labourers, and possibly as 'apostle' (though there is much discussion about Junia[s]). Is the system of church order in the New Testament an example of how it *can* be, or an institution of how it *should* be for all time?

The book is divided into two parts, Part 1 dealing with the whole area of women as 'woman, wife and mother'. This is followed by a discussion in Part 2 of women in ministry, in the church. You will note that the somewhat specialized and much discussed subject of ordination of women has been left aside. This has been deliberate so as not to overshadow the wider issue of 'ministry'. In each section there are two contributors (a man and a woman) stating a more traditional viewpoint, and two stating a less traditional one. Each contributor has then been given the opportunity of a very brief reply to those with whom he or she differs.

There are areas where our writers remain in disagreement in spite of their determination to submit to Scripture. You will therefore not be able to agree with everything. Some of your ideas may well be modified as you read, as mine have been as I've been involved for several years in the fascinating privilege of editing. There are no easy answers. But read on with an open mind, praying that God will instruct you through his Word. Hopefully we shall all come to a deeper understanding of the problem and a willingness to go on to seek a greater knowledge of God's Word and his will for our lives – whether we are men or women.

SHIRLEY LEES

Part 1

Woman in the home

Headship in marriage:
the husband's view

Mankind: male and female

Husband/wife relationships:
a practical Christian viewpoint

Woman in the home

Elizabeth Catherwood

*Women and marriage · Submission · Submission not
subjugation · Woman with her children and home ·
Pressures of Christian work · Pressures to go out to
work · Use of the home*

Some time ago I was visiting a student in her rooms at
one of our older universities. She was an able, warm-
hearted girl who came from a united and socially caring
family, in which the mother had taken up again an active
academic life once the youngest child had started school.
The girl had established herself as a leader among her
fellow-students and her room was littered with pamphlets
and hand-outs of every protesting kind.

It was her walls that caught my attention. They were
festooned with feminist posters of every kind, and in pride
of place was a wedding cartoon with a bride, a bridegroom
wearing a pig's head, and the caption, 'Wot a waste!'

This cartoon was a gut expression of a viewpoint that
has been gaining ground in past years. Marriage, with its
binding legal contract and its further implication of home
and children, is a shackle from which the modern woman
must break free. Even if marriage is tolerated, there can
be no word more laden with the aura of boredom, lack
of ability and character, or even sheer horror, than that
of 'housewife'.

Recently a leading national daily newspaper published
a list of do's and don'ts for the wife who wants to help
her husband to get on in business. Never, she was told,
must she admit to her husband's boss that she is 'merely

a housewife', even if she has to invent a career for herself on the spot. Yet, frequently, far from furthering her husband's cause, the wife's career can both hinder it and also put the marriage itself into jeopardy. It is increasingly common to meet men living alone, either in this country or overseas in business or diplomatic service, because their wives feel that their own professional advancement would be harmed if they moved with their husband's job.

Rarely has the whole basis of marriage and woman's role as a home-maker been under greater attack than it is today. For the Christian woman in particular this can be a great difficulty, for though not 'of' this world, she has been called to live in it. Often, in insidious ways of which she may not even be conscious, she may find her thoughts and behaviour controlled by the spirit of the age rather than by the biblical pattern for women. Yet, in a society where divorce, one-parent families and juvenile crime are on the increase, perhaps Christian women have, like Esther, been sent to the nation 'for such a time as this'. We must not mind being called 'old-fashioned', 'domestic cabbages', or even 'traitors to the cause', but we must study our Bibles afresh, discover what our God-given role as women is, and fight for that.

In so doing, we must try to show that God's laws for society are never harsh or restricting, but are so planned that those who live by them are happier and more secure than those who spend their time fighting for dominance or self-expression. Perhaps it is above all in the relationships of marriage and the home that we should remind ourselves of the biblical injunction,

> Do nothing from selfishness or conceit, but in humility count others better than yourselves. Let each of you look not only to his own interests, but also to the interests of others (Phil. 2:3–4).

Women and marriage

We need to look first at the relationship of a wife to her husband, and then, secondly, to her children.

So much of the stridency of the current debate on this vital subject has undoubtedly arisen from the appalling subjugation of women practised by sinful men throughout the ages. The times when a wife was legally the chattel of her husband, when she had no control over her property or even over her own children, are now, in Western countries at least, mercifully almost entirely behind us, but much of the bitterness remains. 'Equality in society must first mean equality in marriage' is the cry; and great and justifiable benefit has come to women through the legislation that has been passed.

Tragically, much of the harm in the past was done in the name of Christianity. As with many heresies, the harm was done because biblical teaching was twisted and thrown into imbalance. It is therefore important that Christians should carefully study the Bible, to find out exactly what it says. A middle-aged wife told me how, having been brought up in a home where her father was an unreasonable despot, she had decided never to get married. However, when presented with an attractive prospective husband, she had diligently searched the Scriptures to find the truth about marriage, and found that her father's views had been a travesty of divine teaching; that a Christian wife should not be a cowed domestic drudge with no mind, pleasures or money of her own. The Bible makes it clear that all Christians must submit to one another, that husbands must love their wives as Christ loved the church (Eph. 5:21); they must treat their wives with respect, as the weaker partner and as heirs with them of the gracious gift of life (1 Pet. 3:7).[1]

Right from the beginning the Bible makes it clear that woman was created for man. 'The Lord God said, "It is

---

[1] We need to have this teaching for husbands always in our minds. The biblical balance is perfect. But this book is written from the woman's angle, and its emphases must therefore be those which concern her in particular. In passing, it is interesting to observe that, in a desire to compensate for the past, many speakers and writers on this subject so emphasize the errors on the man's part, that some young men are almost afraid of taking up a leadership position in the family. The results are often unsettling for all concerned.

not good that the man should be alone; I will make him a helper fit for him" ' (Gn. 2:18). Paul underlines this when he says, 'neither was man created for woman, but woman for man' (1 Cor. 11:9); and he goes on to make it clear that this divine purpose in woman's creation in no way makes her an inferior being. That is the tragic error made in so many other religions. In the introduction to this book we have seen already how in creation in the image of God, in salvation and in all the blessings of the Christian life, men and women are equal, as they should be, too, in all the freedoms of daily life and living.

It is however a fact which is rapidly becoming neglected, even in Christian circles, that the wife's primary concern is to be someone who, in every way, is a help to her husband (Gn. 2:18). This is illustrated by the remarkable woman of Proverbs 31. It is however interesting that as a helper she is clearly someone who runs her family and household so efficiently that her husband is free to take his place as a leader in the outside world. He is 'respected at the city gate, where he takes his place among the elders of the land'. Furthermore, because she fulfils her role so well, not only do her husband and children praise her, but her works bring *her* praise at the city gate as well.

The Christian wife is a helper to her husband physically, emotionally, mentally and spiritually. The wife of Proverbs 31 is commended as much for her wise speech as she is for her domestic competence. The apostle Paul (often unjustly maligned for his attitude towards women) makes it clear in 1 Corinthians 7 that men and women have equal marital rights. But while in these days of Women's Lib. one often hears of ruthlessly demanding husbands, how often is it shown that the unfairly withholding wife is equally unkind?

Above all, she is to be a helper spiritually, not only to her Christian husband with whom she is a joint heir of God's grace, but in some marriages the husband may be helped to belief in Christ by the 'purity and reverence' of her life (1 Pet. 3:2). We must reiterate, being a helper does not make her inferior. She is the complement of the man.

Therefore the wife should rejoice in her position. She has been made by God to help man to function as God's representative in this world. She is to be his comforter, the one to whom he can speak and look for comfort and encouragement. . . . Man realizes the truth about himself, she also realizes the truth about herself, and thus she complements and aids him; and together they live to the glory of God and the Lord Jesus Christ.[2]

Submission

The way in which she is to fulfil this role is also emphasized in Scripture. And here we come to the question of 'submission', that difficult word which has often caused women much agony of mind. Paul in Ephesians exhorts wives to submit to their husbands in everything 'as to the Lord', an expression that has given rise to some misunderstanding. Some have interpreted this as meaning that the wife's attitude to her husband is the same as her attitude to Christ. But this is obviously going too far, because the submission of every believer (male or female) to the Lord Jesus Christ is to be absolute. Clearly, this verse takes us back to the preceding one where we are told to submit to one another 'in the fear of Christ'. In the last analysis, it is not for the sake of the husband that the wife submits. It is for the sake of Christ, the Lord who has given her this role to fulfil, as a picture of the church in her relationship to the one who loved the church and gave himself for her. As John Stott says in *God's New Society*: 'Behind the husband . . . [she] must discern the Lord himself who has given him his authority.'[3] Colossians 3:18 makes all this abundantly clear. 'Wives, be subject to your husbands, *as is fitting in the Lord*.'

In a way, the apostle Peter expresses the teaching on the wife's submission even more strongly. In his first epistle, in the context of the Christian's submission to every

---

[2] D. M. Lloyd-Jones, *Life in the Spirit – in Marriage, Home and Work* (Banner of Truth, 1974).

[3] J. R. W. Stott, *God's New Society* (IVP, 1979), p. 218.

authority instituted among men and of slaves' submission to their masters, he writes, '*Likewise* you wives, be submissive to your husbands' (1 Pet. 3:1), even when the husband is not a Christian. Later in the passage, with reference to Sarah, he even employs the word for *obey* which Paul applies only to children and slaves.

Now in case modern women should feel that submission is a problem peculiar to them in this emancipated age, we should realize that the very presence of those admonitions in letters written to the early churches shows that they were necessary then as well. Even earlier, Solomon – perhaps inevitably – had problems with a woman who was like 'a continual dripping on a rainy day' (Pr. 27:15), while on occasion he hankered after a corner of a roof in preference to a house shared with a quarrelsome wife (Pr. 21:9).

Most women at all times have not found submission easy. (Here, however, we should remember that Paul's exhortations to men are infinitely more awe-inspiring and demanding). But as Christian women we must not allow ourselves to react violently according to the spirit of the age. We must carefully consider the whole context in which such teaching is given. We must not, in modern liberal fashion, ascribe the New Testament views of submission to first-century male arrogance on the part of Peter and Paul. To quote John Stott again: 'This is not chauvinism, but creationism.'[4] Biblically it is a matter, as we have seen, of different roles laid down by God for man and woman in the beginning. Tragically, the fall brought in a new dimension. In some ways, part of Eve's original sin was that she took the lead in the confrontation with the devil. 'Adam was not the one deceived,' says Paul; 'it was the woman who was deceived and became a sinner' (1 Tim. 1:14). She took over, and led man into sin, and one of the solemn results was that the complementary headship of the husband was turned into the divine judgment, 'he shall rule over you' (Gn. 3:16).

This biblical history is shown by Paul to be the basis of

[4] *Ibid.*, p. 221.

his teaching with regard to women and authority, and it is a fact which women must always recognize and accept.

But mercifully the whole of the passage in Ephesians 5 is irradiated with the doctrine of the atonement. The wife is a picture of the church, the bride of Christ, whom he loved so much that he died for her. 'In the same way', Paul demands, almost incredibly, 'must a man love his wife.' But what an encouragement to the wife, to give her whole-hearted devotion to the one with whom she has become one flesh! The word in verse 16 which the NIV translates *respect* is stronger in the original, including as it does the sense of 'fear'. The AV *reverence* is perhaps nearer the mark with its feeling, not of craven fear, but of deference.

James Hurley gives an excellent illustration of a Christian wife's attitude in *Man and Woman in Biblical Perspective*. In a difficult situation where she cannot agree with her husband's course of action, he suggests that in effect what she says is this:

> Not because I believe you are wiser in this matter (I don't) or more righteous, nor because I accept that you are right (because I don't or I would not oppose you), but because I am a servant of God who has called me to honour your headship, I willingly yield to your decision. If I am wrong, may God show me. If you are wrong, may he give you grace to acknowledge it and to change.[5]

We are living in a world riddled with a desire for self-expression and an insistence on one's 'rights', and Christian women are constantly under every kind of pressure. 'Do what is right and do not give way to fear,' urges Peter (1 Pet. 3:6, NIV), writing, as we have seen, partly to women whose husbands are not Christians. Be 'like Sarah', he encourages them, and like 'the holy women of the past'. Yes, they concentrated on self — but it was the 'inner self, the unfading beauty of a gentle and quiet spirit, which is

[5] J. B. Hurley, *Man and Woman in Biblical Perspective* (Inter-Varsity Press, 1981), p. 151.

of great worth in God's sight' (1 Pet. 3:4, NIV).

We Christian women should read and re-read such passages, and ask God to forgive us for being overcome by the too-confident and strident feminist spirit of the times.

> Should not the wife [writes John Stott] even rejoice that she has the privilege of giving a particular demonstration in her attitude to her husband of the beauty of humility which is to characterize all members of God's new society?[6]

Furthermore, to help us on our way, Paul reminds us that our submission is *voluntary*. Perhaps it should be said that unless the Christian woman is prepared to do this, it is better for her not to get married, for the unsubmissive wife is contrary to God's pattern and is actually committing sin. Paul, having said in 1 Corinthians 11 that the head of the woman is the man, goes on to say not only that men must submit to the headship of Christ, but also – marvellously – that the head of Christ is God. What greater parallel could there be for women? He who 'was in the form of God, did not count equality with God a thing to be grasped' (Phil. 2:6), yet, in order to bring about our salvation, submitted himself totally to the Father and could say, 'I seek not my own will but the will of him who sent me' (Jn. 5:30).

So often when considering woman as a 'helper', or her submission, or her supportive role, people ask for exact definitions or specific details as to *how* she is to carry these out in modern society. But when speaking of this relationship, the Bible lays down the general principles and leaves us to work out the details for ourselves. Things do tend, in spite of their difficulty and complexity, to fall into perspective when we ask ourselves whether our attitude to our head (man) is as like as possible to the Son's attitude to the Father, his Head. Anyway, details may alter from case to case and are likely to cause confusion in a discussion because people tend to latch on to

---

6 J. R. W. Stott, *God's New Society*, p. 233.

a particular point instead of dealing with the main thrust of the argument. Furthermore, as we shall see, biblical history provides us with many helpful examples.

Submission not subjugation

One of the chief problems in this discussion on women's submission is that we immediately tend to see in it the end of all our personalities, characters, and even powers of speech and action.[7] However, nowhere in the New Testament do women appear to be reduced to brainless ciphers. Submission is not subjugation.

A woman like Priscilla clearly worked with and supported her husband in every way. She was obviously a great character, frequently even referred to before her husband Aquila; she was clear in her understanding of Christian truth, joined with Aquila in putting Apollos right, was a practical support in the job of tent making and seems to have been an outstanding person in the church. Euodia and Syntyche must both have been strong-minded, active ladies, and it is interesting to see that though they were creating difficulties in the church, Paul in no way treats them with the heavy hand of masculine authority. He pleads with them, as he always does in every situation, to remember that they should be living 'in the Lord'.

Then again, the touching references in Paul's letters to 'my dear friend Persis', to the mother of Rufus, to Tryphena and Tryphosa 'who work hard in the Lord', to Apphia, Eunice, Lois and others, all show that he who taught feminine submission as 'fitting in the Lord' both loved and respected the women among whom he worked.

In the Old Testament, too, the women play a considerable part. Deborah, 'the wife of Lappidoth', when confronted by a dithering Barak – a man who refused to

---

[7] All good commentaries on Ephesians, Colossians and 1 Peter bring out the New Testament balance at this point. Perhaps they should be read carefully by those men who are part of the evangelical backlash against the women's liberation movement, who are so keen on 'submission' that they forget the word 'cherish'.

carry out God's call to leadership by himself – responded perfectly. She agreed to go with him, but pointed out his failure and consequent loss of honour (Jdg. 4:4–5). Manoah's wife, by her sound common sense, helped her husband to recognize God's dealings with them (Jdg. 13:23); the Shunammite wife behaved both as a practical hostess and later as a woman of faith (2 Ki. 4); Moses' mother and Rahab acted and spoke with strength and wisdom (Ex. 2; Jos. 2), while Ruth, with her unswerving loyalty and devotion to the people of God, took her place beside her husband as a fore-runner of the royal Davidic line.

God's women have their opinions, remonstrate with their husbands, give advice, think quickly, act with vigour and determination and show many of the qualities so dear to the women's movement; and those things are open to us too. But the Bible must be seen as a whole, and we – and our husbands – must act within the bounds laid down for us in its pages. To strike the right balance is not easy. The very closeness of the marriage relationship can lead to tensions and problems (Paul's picture of the yoke – 'Do not be yoked together with unbelievers' (2 Cor. 6:14, NIV) emphasizes this). There are bound to be times of difficulty, but if the Christian's desire is that God may be glorified in the marriage, then the relationships of life are enlightened by his enabling love and power. This is not a cliché. It has been shown time and time again by people whose marriages were on the verge of breaking down; as they have faced the problems honestly together in the light of God's Word, helped perhaps by wise Christian advice, then their lives together have begun again and their union has been renewed.

The difficulties are perhaps exacerbated today by the debasement and misuse of the word 'love'. In an article recently in a national newspaper on what people should do when they 'fall in love' outside their marriage, the writer commented,

> Love is in fact anarchic, it recognises no rules, it obeys no commands and it accepts no ethic. Indeed the only

ethic which we can ourselves impose, is either to refuse to live where we love (if the person we love seems in other ways unsuitable or reprehensible) or to decide to live where we do not love (for the sake of the children, or a principle of duty or even fear, insecurity or greed). This means living by other imperatives than love and may, at times, have much to recommend it, as long as we are aware of what we do.

In this passage, love tends to be equated totally with what the younger generation refers to as 'fancying'. It is an instinctive reaction, which, of course, Christians too recognize and rejoice in – the sexual attraction, the 'mysterious chemistry' which is present when two people are drawn to each other. One Christian does not marry another simply because they are Christians – though this has been a dangerous pitfall for some. Compatibility of character and interests, too, needs to be present, but – and it is a big but – according to the Bible, love is not anarchic. We need only read 1 Corinthians 13 to see that love must obey commands and accept an ethic. The principle of duty is not 'another imperative than love'; we are enjoined, as part of our wifely love, to be faithful to, to help and to submit to our husbands. In a way it is only by accepting this ethic that we can ultimately fully love.

But are there no limits to the wife's submission? What abut mental breakdown on the husband's part? Here I am reminded of a conversation between a wise older woman – an admirable example of a Christian wife – and a restive younger married girl. 'What would you do', the latter asked, triumphantly producing a *reductio ad absurdum*, 'if your husband woke you in the middle of the night and insisted that you went out and posted a letter for him? Would you obey him?' 'Yes,' replied the older lady, 'I would.' Then she paused and added, 'But I would make sure that I phoned the doctor in the morning.'

She was surely right. Christianity must never be ridiculous; a mentally sick husband needs medical help, not slavish obedience.

31

Again, the Christian wife should never be put by her husband into the position of going against her own conscience or causing her relationship with Christ to suffer. 'We must obey God rather than men' (Acts 5:29), said Peter to the Sanhedrin, and ultimately the woman's chief loyalty is to the Lord himself.

Abigail is an interesting biblical illustration of this. Realizing that David was God's man – 'The Lord will certainly make a lasting dynasty for my master, because he fights the Lord's battles' (1 Sa. 25:28, NIV) – she supported him in every way, even though her husband, Nabal, had been uncooperative.

Yet the wife should not use this as an excuse to take a stand on what is actually only a matter of her own opinion. I know a wife who cheerfully wears a hat to meetings because her husband feels strongly about it, though she herself does not feel it is at all necessary to do so. Or again, I have known a non-Christian husband whose heart was softened by his Christian wife's preparedness to forgo one of the Sunday services in order to keep him company. Peter's advice is deeply helpful in this sphere, though perhaps it should be underlined that, in the biblical context, he is speaking to Christian wives who are *already* married to an unbelieving husband. The whole weight of scriptural teaching is that a Christian should not marry a non-Christian – 'Can two walk together, except they be agreed?' (Am. 3:3, AV); 'Do not be yoked together with unbelievers. . . . What does a believer have in common with an unbeliever?' (2 Cor. 6:14–15, NIV). For all the reasons we have been considering, it is tragic and sinful folly for a Christian woman deliberately to enter into a marriage relationship which calls her to submit to and obey one who is not a servant of Christ. I say 'deliberately' because there are remarkable stories of Christian women in other countries who have been forced to marry men of another faith, where the Lord has gloriously undertaken for them. In underlining Christian principles, one must allow for certain exceptions. God is more gracious than we are, and often hyper-legalism on our part may be put to shame. But, on the other hand, in almost every circumstance the biblical teachings and principles are there for our guidance and obedience. We neglect them at our peril.

One last difficult area for the Christian wife is to know just what her role is when confronted with an adulterous husband. Does she still submit to him? Is the same behaviour required of her, or is there a change in the whole relationship because of his conduct? Christ's words in Matthew 18 show (though this has been an area of disagreement among Christians) that it is adultery alone which breaks up a marriage. The 'one flesh' has been severed by the fact of one of the partners joining themselves to a third person, and 'for the hardness of heart' of sinful men and women, Moses, as God's lawgiver, allowed divorce in such circumstances. It would seem, then, that for a woman who finds herself in this tragic situation and who feels that divorce is the right course for her to take, the obligations of a wife no longer pertain to her.

Woman with her children and home

Paul, in writing to Titus, gives a most helpful synopsis of the married woman's priorities. It is always fascinating to see how relevant the biblical message is to all periods of history. The older women, clearly finding time on their hands, are urged not to waste their time in gossiping – the deadly canker in so many churches – nor in too much drinking (another temptation for middle-aged, under-occupied women). Instead they are urged to realize their responsibilities in showing younger women their role in society and how they can best fulfil it.

The husband, as we have been seeing, comes first. Then Paul moves on to the other areas of a wife's life, her children and her home. In 1 Timothy 5, too, in enumerating the essential qualities of the 'list of widows', he gives as her first 'good deed', 'bringing up children'. Throughout the Bible, while the final authority is clearly accorded to the father, it is the mother who is shown as being the one who is intimately involved in caring for the children. The Proverbs 31 'woman of noble character'; Hannah; even the wife who misuses her motherhood, like Leah or Rebekah, and many others illustrate this point; and it is interesting to see how God provides Moses with his own mother to look after him, even in the court of Pharaoh. Verses in the Old Testament such as Isaiah 49:15 underline it further: 'Can a mother forget the baby at her breast and have no compassion on the child she has borne?' The prophet seems to imply that such a thought should be inconceivable, but if even this should happen, then mercifully the Lord's promise is, 'I will not forget you.' Or, 'As a mother comforts her child, so will I comfort you' (Is. 66:13); again the note of the caring closeness of the bond between mother and children. Motherhood, as the Bible lays it before us, is the other great way for a wife to fulfil her God-given purpose.

We see this illustrated in 1 Timothy 2:15. Paul, having laid down his standards for women's appearance and place in the church, then takes us back, as we have seen, to the story of creation and the fall. Then, having shown where she went wrong, he shows how God's blessing will be upon her if she lives her life according to God's pattern. The difficulty in the verse arises from the allusion to childbirth. Some commentators feel that this should be translated 'kept safe through childbirth if she continues . . .'; but what of the countless godly wives throughout history who for a variety of medical reasons have died in childbirth? Is it suggested that their faith and holiness were lacking? Many other commentators reject this explanation totally (for example, R. C. H. Lenski in his commentary on 1 Timothy states that the verb 'saved' 'has its full soteriological meaning'); while the NIV, which uses it, carefully gives the alternative rendering 'be saved' also. Other interpretations suggest the possibility of an elliptical reference to *the* childbirth of Christ through Mary 'the seed of the woman', or again a reminder, as in 1 Corinthians 11:12, that man must remember that he is 'born of woman' and must therefore not be proud against her. But whatever one's understanding of the verse may be, it is clear that Paul is emphasizing that God's purpose for *womanhood*, in spite of her sin in the fall, is that she should be honoured for this, her unique role.

At this point the whole place and purpose of the un-married woman must arise, and also perhaps those of the married woman who has no children. In no way can the verse be interpreted as suggesting that the bearing of children is essential to a godly life. For the unmarried woman, 1 Corinthians 7 is the most helpful passage, but this is a study which belongs to other parts of this book, because here we are discussing the woman's role within marriage.

It would seem to me to be also necessary to sound a caveat against the pitfall contained in the introduction to the Marriage Service in the Elizabethan Book of Common Prayer. Its statement that 'First, [marriage] was ordained for the procreation of children, to be brought up in the fear and nurture of the Lord', hardly agrees with the verse in Genesis that we have considered. 'It is not good for the man to be alone. I will make a helper suitable for him' (Gn. 2:18). Surely the 'mutual society, help and comfort that the one ought to have of the other', later referred to in the service, should have come first. Many couples, knowing that for a variety of reasons they could not have children and yet wanting to marry, were made unneces-sarily anxious by this preamble. Of course, the wider rami-fications of a similar misunderstanding of the scriptural order can be seen in much of the Roman Catholic teaching on marriage and childbearing.

Yet, having said all that, there does seem to be a growing tendency among Christian couples to decide not to have children, often for such reasons as the one described by a young wife in a discussion group: 'I'm not mad about children anyway; we've both got interesting jobs, and if we had kids, they probably wouldn't have much of a life, because we really would resent having them.' Or, in order that every home comfort can be first acquired, having a baby is put off for so long that when it does arrive there *is* a certain resentment at the curtailing of freedom.

Obviously there is a balance needed. The pre-family planning days in which the mother's health and strength were ruined by over-frequent babies are now a thing of the past in many countries, and where there is a lack of money, wisdom and advice are needed to protect the family from being too big for the finances to support. But everywhere the Bible speaks of children as being God's blessing – 'children a reward from him', 'Blessed is the man whose quiver is full of them' (Ps. 127:3, 5, NIV). God's promises are to his people and their children (Ezk. 37:25); and the whole Old Testament picture is one of God dealing with his people, who in their turn pass his words and his ways on to their children. The family is seen as God's special unit, and as evangelicals we need to beware of the modern individualistic tendency which dismisses this as a primitive society organizing itself. It is true that in one sense our family is the church, but the human family is God's ordinance; when God the Son came to the world, he came to a woman with a husband and into a home which later had brothers and sisters. Though they often failed to understand him, as a child 'He was obedient to them' and at the end he cared for his mother and made provision for her. Then, as we have seen, the family is an integral part of Paul's practical teaching to the churches, not only in his advice on the roles of husbands, wives and children, but even more widely: 'If anyone does not provide for his relatives, and especially for his immediate family, he has denied the faith and is worse than an unbeliever' (1 Tim. 5:8, NIV).

The Christian, then, in these tragic and insecure days, must fight for the existence of God's great gift, the family, and here, above all, the God-fearing woman has a part of tremendous importance. The father's role, biblically, is clearly vital; he is the final authority, the lover and cherisher of the mother, the wisely disciplining, non-provoking, caring, compassionate head of the little group. But as we here concentrate on the mother, we can see that, after her husband, her children are her chief concern.

Sometimes, however, and this is often among women who are most anxious to serve God faithfully, there can be a misunderstanding along this very line. A true story of a little boy aged six away at a boarding school illustrates this. One evening, bed-time stories were being discussed, and the child commented, 'My mummy is much too busy with the Lord's work to tell me bed-time stories.'[8] Surely, for the Christian mother, the 'Lord's work' *is* her children. Husband and wife as two adults can sometimes together decide to sacrifice themselves in their Christian service. But this often demands sacrifices from their children of a lack of the mother's presence and direct care. These are sacrifices which they should never be called upon to make, and which (in spite of parental protestations that all is well) they cannot possibly understand.

Pressures of Christian work

Many sensitive issues arise out of this and ones which are often discussed among Christians. The children of missionaries must be one of them. I well remember the fierce little daughter of some missionary friends saying, 'You probably read that article about our school where it says that Mr and Mrs X were like a mummy and daddy to us. Well they're *not*. They couldn't be.' A diplomatic wife once told me how hard she had had to fight to keep her children with her on her husband's various postings, and how grateful she had been to American missionary wives in several places who had cheerfully set up schools for their children with postal help from home.

Perhaps in this country, in both secular and Christian spheres, much more thought is needed on the subject. Is education, British or otherwise, really more important than the mother's immediate care? If the climate is very bad for young children, should parents be sent there as workers at all? Perhaps more consideration should be given to the possibility of parents being sent home during the children's formative years (mercifully, an increasing practice) or to the setting up of many more, smaller,

[8] An article was written in the Graduates' Fellowship magazine some years ago, called 'Evangelical Widows', in which the pathetic plight was described of many Christian wives, left neglected and alone night after night to cope with the stresses of young family life, while the husbands were out and about doing 'the Lord's work'. Perhaps, at some point, another article on 'Evangelical Orphans' should be written.

schools in a more *ad hoc* fashion, as is done by other countries, or to the use of local schools wherever possible – though in many areas this might be difficult. There is no easy solution, but we should not be bound by any tradition, educational, cultural or otherwise.

Examples are often quoted where the children accepted the situation happily and showed no scars, but they can be more than equally matched by those who, to quote some wise words by John Ray, an IFES staff worker, 'have sadly rejected Christ and, if asked, will place some of the onus for this on a lack of sensitivity by zealous, often well-meaning parents'. Except when death or serious illness makes parental care impossible, we should never be pushed into seeking a substitute for the loving presence of parents, especially, when the children are younger, for that of the mother.

But in case the non-missionaries among us become too relaxed, what about the mother who is so busy taking meetings, organizing coffee mornings, or filling the house with the needy of every kind, that her home has become like a holiday beach? Children in these circumstances too can be neglected, or even physically pushed out. Dr Jane Hogbin in an excellent article (*In the Service of Medicine*, July 1976) quotes a mother: 'We will have to send our daughter to a good school, as we do not have the time to encourage her in all the activities other children do.' John Ray also comments that we must be 'aware of the very real tensions that can be generated where the parents are zealous in the Lord's work and growing children feel and sometimes resent what they see as intrusions into the home.' Furthermore, all I have said about missionaries' children can apply to children from Christian homes in this country sent away to boarding schools for most of the year. (Perhaps another book in this series is called for!)

Pressures to go out to work

Of course 'the Lord's work' is by no means the only problem for the mother. The growing pressure to have a job can almost make us feel guilty if we make our home our chief sphere of activity. In many cases it is clear that the mother must work to help keep the family. Death or illness of the father, divorce, unemployment and, shamefully, underpayment of Christian workers, all play their part in forcing some mothers to be full or partial breadwinners. There are also, however, some who feel that they must work in order to obtain for the family as high a standard of living as possible, a real problem, particularly for children who must keep up with the Joneses at all costs. Dr Hogbin comments:

> Surely, as Christians, we should be prepared to challenge the idea that material possessions are of greater importance to the family than the presence of the mother at home.

There can be no hard and fast rules here; the well-off should not adjudicate for the less well-off or vice versa, but Christians need to consider all the aspects of such a decision on spiritual as well as financial grounds.

It is not only the need for money that drives the mother out to work. Much of the pressure comes in the form of encouragement to the married woman to 'do her own thing', to express her 'real self' and not to allow her abilities and training to atrophy. Clearly there is a great deal in this. Many a mother, as she washes the tenth football/hockey shirt, breaks her back looking under the furniture for the missing blue rabbit so vital for comfort and sleep (not to speak of family peace), assures her teenage daughter that two spots on her chin do not mean an irrevocable barrier to future marriage prospects, or adjudicates between the rival merits of two pop groups, may well wonder why on earth she has a physics or history degree or a high-powered secretarial qualification. It is a real tonic to stop talking about Peter Rabbit, that 'horrible' Sarah/Dave – or even the machinations of macro/micro economics – and just be involved for a time with her own skills and interests. The truly caring and supportive husband will encourage her to develop those, but she on her part needs to be very sure of her priorities. Is she sure that she is not doing this to assert her own importance, in a spirit of not seeing why she should be restricted by the children? Does her career matter more to her than the well-being of her husband and children? Is she forgetting that her primary role is that of helpmeet?

Part-time work is the answer for many. Some women, modern versions of Proverbs 31, seem able to run immaculate houses, have marvellous, gifted children, take Open University degrees, have jobs, do all the dressmaking, produce excellent chutney, *etc.*, *etc.*, in a way that leaves us lesser breeds gasping. In the end, of course, every woman can only herself decide her own capacities. But she needs to be really honest with herself and to be quite sure that her husband and children are not suffering. Dr Hogbin again observes:

> The attribute that appears to be in shortest supply in our modern society is *time*. That is precisely what the full-time mother has to offer – time to listen, *time to be there* to offer comfort to her family. . . . Although the mother does have more free time once the children have started school, it is limited by the need to be there and free to listen when the children come home [My italics].

That last point would seem to me to be of the utmost importance. Of course the extreme of the suffocating, possessive, dominant mother, who, having no interests of her own, fixates herself upon the doings of her family, is a much to be avoided horror.[9] But the sympathetic, cheering, encouraging mother at the end of the day, when the teacher has been more diabolical than usual (I speak as a teacher myself) or 'the others' have all misunderstood, or one is just tired by the whole process of living, is of infinite value.

---

[9] A similar problem is presented by the wife who, not content with providing a good back-up service, insists on involving herself with her husband's job on virtually equal terms. In some occupations this may be possible, though even then the wife must be careful not to become a source of embarrassment either to her husband or to others. A husband and a wife are a team. But not everybody can be a centre-forward; the goalkeeper has an essential part to play as well.

Use of the home

The whole question of time, also, brings in the tremendous use that the wife can make of her home. In a way, this is her kingdom. It is interesting, incidentally, to see how the woman of Proverbs 31 appears to be firmly based at home; with the assistance of her helpers and staff, she seems to hold all the threads from the centre, and, considering all she gets done in the household, one would not think that she actually travels like the merchant ships, but organizes all the exports and imports from the domestic harbour.

Also, she 'extends her hands to the needy' and, with the caveat already mentioned, how important it is that there should be Christian women, not tied down by regular jobs, mainly at home, who are free for the many needy people to be found in the modern world. The elderly, the housebound, overseas students, the ill, the depressed, and many more, all need help or a listening ear; and just a bit of time can make all the difference. Some women speak of how lonely and bored they would be without a job. The Christian housewife who takes to heart Paul's exhortation, 'Carry each other's burdens' (Gal. 6:2), even though she may be pressurized for not having a 'fulfilling' career, can be encouraged to know that in Paul's eyes she is fulfilling the law of Christ.

There is an endless need for people with a little 'free' time. In fact, as Dr Hogbin says, we have become too brainwashed by modern thought: 'We are bombarded with articles full of advice for "working" wives and we come to accept that wives who stay at home do nothing' – or perhaps worse, that the only ones who really help in the community are the professionals, social workers, teachers, nurses, *etc*. In this context, we must not let even the menial tasks put us off. The older widows in 1 Timothy 5 are commended for 'washing the feet of the saints', and the general principle surely must be that we must be prepared to see to the well-being of other people, even down to details.

Hospitality (within the limitations mentioned earlier) is an invaluable area for Christian love and witness. Many a Christian woman (here, too, the unmarried are included) has seen it as her special sphere of service which can be used and blessed of God. Paul exhorts the women in the churches of Timothy and Titus to 'manage their homes', and to be 'busy at home'; and R. C. H. Lenski in his commentary on Titus says,

> [The home's] greatness and its importance should ever be held up as woman's divinely intended sphere, in which all her womanly qualities and gifts find full play and happiest gratification.

Husband, children, home, other people, her own interests; all these are the Christian woman's life, lived within the great circle of her Saviour's love for her and her desire to serve him. We must not let the world unbalance our scriptural priorities. We must rejoice in our calling, and we must not be afraid of being called old-fashioned – or worse. In answer to a lady who said recently on the radio, 'All this talk about different roles for men and women is a load of rubbish,' we must be prepared to rise up and shout back with undiminished vigour, 'Oh, no it isn't!'

Headship in marriage: the husband's view

David Field

Reluctant heads · The Bible and feminism ·
The culture question · The meaning of headship ·
Getting it together

'Grace and peace in Christ – and authority over your wife.' That was how Martin Luther once began a letter to a friend, Stephen Roth. We are not told how Mr Roth reacted to this greeting, nor whether he dared show the letter to Mrs Roth afterwards. As citizens of the sixteenth century perhaps neither of them thought the wording at all odd. Luther himself might have been puzzled to learn that his greeting would have provoked either laughter or embarrassment at the average Christian breakfast-table four hundred years later.

The whole idea of a husband wielding authority over his wife leaves a nasty taste in modern mouths. The truth is that many husbands today feel just as uncomfortable as their emancipated wives do about the old-style authoritarian patterns of married life. And there are several powerful social reasons why this should be so.

Reluctant heads

There is, in the first place, the relatively new emphasis on *the relational values of marriage*. As twentieth-century Christians we may find no problems in thinking of marriage first and foremost as a partnership, but a glance at the church history books is enough to show that the

43

roots of sexism go very deep in this respect. Even John Calvin, who stressed the relational aspect of marriage far more strongly than most of his predecessors, described woman as 'a kind of appendage' and a 'lesser helpmeet' who 'by nature is born to obey'.

Today we live on the other side of a social revolution as far as our understanding of marriage is concerned. Few modern husbands see their wives as household slaves, even if some are occasionally guilty of treating them that way. So it is only natural that the man of the house should feel less and less comfortable when he is asked to perform the traditional role of lord and master.

The feminist movement has made an important contribution to the chauvinist's discomforture too. However much its critics may deplore its excesses, feminism has been very successful indeed in exposing the way men can use their inherited position of privilege to demean the opposite sex.

Advertisers regularly display women as sex-objects. Successful business women find that men resent their 'unnatural' competition. Wives who stay at home have to confess that they 'just' do housework. Exposure of contemporary social attitudes like these has provoked valid criticism from the feminist camp, and modern husbands with any social conscience at all deplore this kind of sexual exploitation just as strongly as their wives. It is hardly surprising that many react by rejecting the authoritarian role that has apparently spawned it.

There is also a third, less honourable factor: *the erosion of personal responsibility*. We live in times when it is more fashionable to shelve responsibility than to take it. Inasmuch as accepting authority implies accepting responsibility, there are many husbands who are only too willing for their wives to make all the choices and take all the decisions. Life is nearly always easier that way – assuming, of course, that they (the husbands) are free to 'do their own thing' in the meantime.

For all those reasons – and others – modern husbands can feel just as uneasy as their wives do about accepting the authority role which their grandfathers would have assumed as their right. For every married man who has been pushed off the domestic throne against his will, there are three or four others who have simply and gladly abdicated.

The Bible and feminism

Here, however, the Christian feels uneasy for different reasons. It is all very well for a twentieth-century husband to surrender his authority with a sigh of relief, but doesn't the Bible teach us that the man should always be head of the home? And if the Bible is God's Word, ought not Christians to be fighting the permissive spirit of the age, instead of giving it a nod of approval? Unpopular though the thought may be, should we not be campaigning to reinstate headship in marriage?

The most casual reading of the New Testament does seem to confirm the husband in his role as head. Paul, for example, backs his call to Christian women at Ephesus to submit to their husbands by insisting that 'the husband is the head of the wife as Christ is the head of the church' (Eph. 5:23). And he echoes the same theme in his letter to the Colossians: 'Wives, submit to your husbands' (Col. 3:18, NIV). Peter, too, strikes a similar note. He even brackets subordination with obedience as he encourages his female readers to be 'submissive . . . like Sarah, who obeyed Abraham and called him her master' (1 Pet. 3:1, 5–6, NIV).

Yet the Bible is far from being an anti-feminist manifesto. We can, in fact, trace many echoes of our contemporary feminists' major complaints in the pages of Scripture. When it comes to exposing chauvinism, the Bible is often to be found on the side of the critics.

Status
As far as status is concerned, for example, Scripture strongly opposes the view that husbands are superior to wives. Right from the story of creation, the Bible is very firm in its insistence on the equality of the sexes. 'God created man in his own image,' writes the author of

Genesis, choosing his words with enormous care; 'in the image of God he created him; male and female he created them' (Gn. 1:27). And over in the New Testament Paul takes up these very words from Genesis when he explains to the Galatians that Jesus Christ has put an end to all discrimination (Gal. 3:28). The label of chauvinist-in-chief which some feminists tie round Paul's neck looks a little silly in the light of a radical broadside like that! The gospel rules out all sexism, along with all racism and all class divisiveness.

Whatever else Paul meant, therefore, in saying that the husband is the wife's 'head', he certainly did not mean that men are in any sense superior to women. Status and headship are quite separate issues as far as the Bible is concerned. The 'head' is sometimes clearly superior to the subordinate (as 'Christ is the head of the church'); sometimes equal in status (as 'the head of Christ is God'); and sometimes even inferior (as when Christ submitted to the authority of Pontius Pilate as Head of State). So when the New Testament says that the husband is the head of his wife it is saying nothing about the *status* of either partner. Nor is it contradicting its own plain statements elsewhere that men and women enjoy absolute equality in their creation in God's image and in their redemption in Christ. Christian feminists such as Letha Scanzoni are being unbiblical, therefore, when they claim that 'equality and subordination are contradictions'. The Bible sees nothing incompatible in headship and equality.

Personhood
The Bible also supports the feminists strongly in insisting that women should be treated as people, not sex-objects. Today, the latter attitude surfaces most obviously in the 'Playboy mentality' that locates the value of a girl in her vital statistics. Further back in history, before the age of contraception and world overcrowding, women were treated more as baby-bearers than as man-pleasers. The symptoms may differ, but the disease is the same. Ancient husbands who looked on their wives as baby-machines were falling into exactly the same trap as their twentieth-

century counterparts who ogle women as playthings.

Far from defending this attitude as a legitimate spin-off from the man's authority-role in creation, the Bible traces it to mankind's fall into sin. Then for the first time, according to the third chapter of Genesis, Adam and his wife were embarrassed by their nudity – because then, for the first time, they became aware of each other as physical specimens instead of as people with physical differences.

It was after sin's arrival, too, that man gave woman a new name – 'Eve, because she would become the mother of all the living' (Gn. 3:20). Innocent though that naming ceremony sounds, it was a clear step backwards from the innocence of Eden. 'Woman', man's partner in the ideal relationship Genesis 2 describes, had now become 'Eve', his means of producing offspring. From now on the temptation to see her as a sex-object, merely a functional aid, would grow stronger and stronger.

God made this shift in perspective explicit when he spelt out the ways sin would spoil marriage. 'Your desire shall be for your husband,' he told Eve, 'and he shall rule over you' (Gn. 3:16).

Some commentators have interpreted that verse positively as an anticipation of the headship assigned to the husband in the New Testament. Ambrose, bishop of Milan in the fourth century, wrote: 'Servitude, therefore, of this sort is a gift of God. Wherefore compliance with this servitude is to be reckoned among blessings.' In its context, however, this 'servitude' is God's curse, not his blessing. Its New Testament parallel does not lie in the man's headship in marriage, but in the oppressive abuse of male authority which Paul highlights when he warns husbands not to be 'harsh' (literally 'embittered') with their wives (Col. 3:19); and which Peter reflects more positively when he writes, 'Husbands . . . be considerate as you live with your wives' (1 Pet. 3:7, NIV).

Balance

Here we come very close to the heart of the Bible's teaching on relationships in marriage. On the one hand, as we have just seen, Scripture joins with the feminist in

condemning sexism in any shape or form. Husbands are
not superior to wives, and women are *not* to be treated
as sex-objects for male exploitation. And yet, on the other
hand, we also find in the Bible a full-blooded assertion
of the very principle which, according to the feminists,
undergirds all sexist oppression – the hierarchical
approach to marriage that makes husbands heads and
requires wives to be subordinate. Are there signs here of
biblical discord?

There is no discord. The harmony is, in fact, very delicately tuned. The two themes interplay. They are carefully
related and finely balanced by the same biblical authors
in the same scriptural passages.

Take Genesis 2, for instance. Man's naming of woman
is a sign of his authority over her (because all naming
symbolized a claim to authority in Old Testament times).
God's intention that she should be 'a helper suitable for
him' (Gn. 2:18) points in a similar direction. And yet in
this same short passage we are told that in the Creator's
plan it is the man who seeks, desires and makes sacrifices
for the woman. So far from being her dominating over-
lord, he will give up anything for her sake. And the 'one
flesh' intimacy they go on to share in marriage leaves no
room for distinctions of superiority and inferiority. They
are simply 'bone of bone and flesh of flesh' together (verse
23). The balance is most carefully struck.

The New Testament exhibits exactly the same harmony.
Peter, for example, describes wives in one breath as
'weaker partners' and in the next as 'heirs with you of the
gracious gift of life' (1 Pet. 3:7). And Paul adds to his bald
statement 'the head of the woman is the man' a balancing
sentence: 'In the Lord, however, woman is not independent of man, nor is man independent of woman' (1 Cor.
11:3, 11, NIV).

Writing to the Ephesians, Paul is even more insistent
that the husband 'is head of the wife' and that wives
'should submit to their husbands' – but is even more
careful, at the same time, to add a balancing command to
husbands to love their wives self-sacrificially (Eph.
5:22–25). Furthermore, he sets both these demands in the

immediate context of an appeal to 'submit to *one another* out of reverence for Christ' (verse 21); and within the broader setting of an explanation of what it means to 'be filled with the Spirit' (verse 18).

Here then is further evidence that in both the Old Testament and the New the themes of headship and interdependence are completely compatible. Both are important elements in a marriage which is lived out in the Spirit of God.

The culture question

Before we go on to explore the meaning of headship more closely, one other line of argument must be considered. Even if Scripture does give a special authority-role to men in marriage, should we not make adjustments for cultural differences before applying this biblical teaching to *modern* marriages? After all, Rebekah's family gave her their blessing to marry Isaac with the words 'May you, sister, become the mother of millions,' but no-one would send a wedding telegram with that message today just because the words come from the Bible. Times have changed!

Was Paul muddled?

The argument can take several different forms, all leading to the same general conclusion. Most radically, some would claim that Paul in particular vacillated between supporting and denying a husband's headship because his Christian ideas about marriage were only half-formed. So C. L. Mitton believes that 'Paul never seems to have quite resolved the conflict between a view of women consistent with his new Christian insights and the view which he inherited from his Jewish past'. The implication is that with greater Christian hindsight we can safely reject the hierarchical half of his teaching on marriage, while gratefully hanging on to the other half which majors on equality and interdependence.

It is difficult to take such a suggestion very seriously. Apart from the grave implications it has for the authority and inspiration of Scripture, it effectively makes Paul seem either an idiot or a muddle-headed communicator. Here was an apostle writing to help living churches with practical problems, and in the course of no less than three of his major letters we find him setting the headship principle alongside the interdependence of husband and wife as two essential elements in Christian marriage. If he was bringing together two incompatible ideas without being aware of it, he was being less than intelligent. And if he *was* aware of the muddle but did nothing about resolving it, he was being at best very careless and at worst dangerously misleading.

All that we know of Paul suggests that he was none of those things. In his mind, if not in ours, there was no muddle at all.

Changing structures
A more acceptable version of the same argument draws our attention to the huge gap that separates the social conditions of Bible times from those of our own. Peter and Paul, it is pointed out, bracketed their teaching on marriage with their teaching on slavery. We no longer expect slaves to obey masters, so why should we ask wives to subject themselves to husbands? The New Testament's teaching accepts – naturally – the social structures of its own day. But now those structures have changed, the old teaching loses its relevance.

This sounds plausible enough, but as an argument it has a fatal flaw. If we are focusing on *structures*, the right parallel to draw is not between slavery and a husband's headship, but between the institution of slavery and the institution of marriage. If our premise is, 'We can ignore the New Testament's teaching on the relationship between masters and slaves because we no longer find slavery acceptable,' our conclusion ought to be, 'We can therefore ignore the New Testament's teaching on the headship of the husband *because we no longer find marriage acceptable*'. There, of course, the analogy breaks down. Scripture presents marriage as a God-ordained institution which must be guarded in its integrity until the end of time. But it makes no such claim for slavery. How, one wonders, would Paul have reacted if a church member at Corinth, having read his advice to slaves in 1 Corinthians 7:21 ('If you can gain your freedom, do so'), then asked innocently whether the same principle might apply to marriage?

Changing expressions
All this is not to pretend that cultural differences do not matter when we apply the Bible's teaching to the issues in today's headlines. They matter very much indeed – so much so that they should always colour the specific applications we make.

Changes of social expression, for example, must be recognized and understood if we are not to draw false conclusions. An English husband might well hesitate before asking his wife to call him 'Master', as Sarah called Abraham (1 Pet. 3:6). Here is an obvious case where we need to make a cultural adjustment. In Bible times such language was no more an expression of servility than it is today when a child in the southern United States calls his parents 'Sir' and 'Ma'am'. But in twentieth-century London both kinds of expression would certainly be misunderstood.

Theological foundations
All of the Bible's teaching is culturally conditioned, in the sense that it was originally directed to real people living in particular places at certain times. But that does not justify us in rejecting its relevance for ourselves. In Stephen Clark's wise words, 'The real issue is this: Among the historically and culturally conditioned teachings we find before us, which have God's authority behind them? Which are expressions of his ways, his character and his purpose for the human race?'[1]

When we examine the New Testament's teaching on the structure of marriage in the light of those questions, we come up with some very interesting answers. The theo-

---

[1] S. B. Clark, *Man and Woman in Christ* (Servant Books, 1980), p. 279.

logical foundations on which the concept of headship is built are dug very deep indeed.

Peter describes the subordination of wives as something 'of great worth in God's sight' (1 Pet. 3:4, NIV). That in itself is enough to take it out of the shifting scene of cultural change.

Paul goes much further than Peter. In Ephesians, he grounds the headship principle on both the Creator's will for all mankind and the Redeemer's example; while in 1 Corinthians he sets marriage's hierarchy alongside the structure of the Godhead itself in a particularly impressive way. His first readers' reactions matched ours, perhaps, as they followed him from the obvious to the almost unbelievable: 'I want you to realize that the head of every man is Christ ["Of course!"], and the head of the woman is man ["Oh dear, here we go again!"], and the head of Christ is God ["*No! Really?*"]' (1 Cor. 11:3).

It would be hard to dream up a more far-reaching doctrinal span to support any biblical command. The principle of headship in marriage is clearly no cultural freak. It is based on theological truths which transcend every imaginable historical and cultural division. As Stephen Clark concludes, 'It is precisely those elements ... that many modern people would like to expunge as time-bound and culturally determined, that Scripture writers considered most central and fundamental.'[2]

Incidentally, the 'culturally conditioned' argument can cut both ways. It is too easily assumed, for example, that the patriarchal structures of Old Testament family life must have frustrated any gifts a wife might have had, beyond our narrow concept of what it takes to keep a home together. Nothing could be further from the truth, as the activities of the 'perfect wife' in Proverbs 31 illustrate. The household in biblical times was the focal point of education, health care, social life and much else. So to say to a wife in those days, 'Your place is in the home,' was to offer her enormous scope for personal fulfilment.

Again it is often taken for granted that Paul is simply

2 S. B. Clark, *op. cit.*, p. 279.

supporting the *status quo* when he insists on a structure of headship and subordination in marriage. But research has revealed the existence of strong feminist movements in both Greek and Roman culture of the first century AD. Ephesus in particular was a well-known bastion of women's rights. So Paul was in fact challenging, not reflecting, local cultural patterns when he wrote to the married members of the Ephesian church, 'Wives, submit to your husbands. . . . For the husband is the head of the wife' (Eph. 5:22–23).

The meaning of headship

If, then, the Bible teaches the principle of headship so clearly – and if its teaching on this theme cannot simply be dismissed as irrelevant to twentieth-century marriages – it becomes all the more important to discover just what 'being head' means.

Here we strike a particularly rich vein of biblical imagery. Before we explore its wealth, however, we must notice one thing 'head' does *not* mean in Scripture. The Hebrews and Greeks had very little knowledge of brain function, so modern phrases like 'a wise head on his shoulders' or 'a head stuffed with knowledge' would have fallen on deaf ears in Bible times. The head was never connected with intelligence. This means that the Bible's teaching on a husband's headship in marriage can never imply that he is the rational member of the partnership. Still less does it suggest that men do the thinking while women only feel!

Apart from its literal meaning, the word 'head' is used in several different ways in the Old Testament. Firstly, it can stand simply for the whole person (as in Numbers 1:2 when Moses was told to 'count heads' in taking a census of Israel). Secondly, it can mean the 'source' or 'beginning' of something like a river, a street or a month (as, *e.g.*, in Gn. 2:10, Ezk. 16:25 and Ex. 12:2). And thirdly, it may signify authority or leadership (as in 'heads of families' and 'heads of the people' in Ex. 6:14 and Jdg. 10:18).

To these three dimensions of meaning we may usefully

add a fourth which is found in extra-biblical Jewish literature. There, the relationship of head to body is sometimes used as a metaphor for unity. This can be illustrated, for example, from the *Testament of Zebulun*, where the author writes: 'Do not divide into two heads; for everything the Lord has made has only one head. He has given two shoulders, hands and feet, but all the members obey one head.'

All four usages are found in the New Testament. Paul's exclamation, 'Your blood be on your own heads!' (Acts 18:6) provides an example of the first. But much more significant, from our point of view, is the way he uses the word 'head' in each of the other three senses we have just identified to describe Christ's relationship to the church. The Lord is the church's head in the sense that he is its *source* (because 'from him ... the whole body grows' – Eph. 4:16). He is also its *unitive principle* (because his headship means 'we are members of his body' – Eph. 5:23, 30). And he is its *focus of authority* (because 'God placed all things under his feet and appointed him to be head over everything for the church' – Eph. 1:22).

The fact that we find the word 'head' applied to Christ with such a rich variety of meaning in Ephesians is particularly significant, because it is in chapter 5 of this same letter that Paul invites husbands to see their marriage role in the light of Christ's headship. 'For the husband is the head of the wife', he writes, 'as Christ is the head of the church, his body' (verse 23). The analogy invites us to understand the husband's headship in the three ways in which Christ's headship has already been described – namely as *source and growth-point*, as *unitive principle* and as focal point of *authority and leadership*. Following these biblical threads, let us explore a little further.

Source and growth-point
In the previous chapter Paul has already described to his Ephesian readers how Christ, as the church's head, is the source of his body's growth. It is from him that the church 'builds itself up in love' (4:16). Now, in chapter 5, he invites Christian husbands to become the source of Christ-

love in their marriages: 'Husbands, love your wives, just as Christ loved the church and gave himself up for her' (verse 25).

The message is clear. Headship, as modelled in Christ, is for service. During his lifetime Jesus took great pains to hammer this point home, both in teaching and by example. He washed his disciples' feet, using the slave's towel to demonstrate what his style of leadership involved (Jn. 13:15). He described himself as their shepherd, his flock's authority figure – but a leader whose chief function would be to serve by giving his life for the sheep (Jn. 10:11). He also contrasted the way secular powers ruled with the way he wanted his followers to exercise their authority; 'the one who rules', he told them, should be 'like the one who serves' (Lk. 22:25–26).

Applied to marriage, a Christian husband fills the role of 'head' most ably when he serves his wife most selflessly. That is the conclusion Paul draws from the pattern of Christ's headship. The husband must lead in self-giving.

This contrasts sharply with the approach of many to marriage today. Ask the average husband why he married his wife, and the chances are he will reply with a 'because' – 'because I found her attractive', perhaps, or 'because she's a marvellous cook'. But if you ask Christ the same question about his bride the church (says Paul), the answer comes back phrased as purpose, not reason (Eph. 5:26–27). Christ's purpose in being Bridegroom and Head is to give, not to get. And that is the pattern Paul prescribes for Christian husbands to follow in relating to their wives.

This, no doubt, is why all the New Testament's teaching on headship in marriage is phrased in the language of responsibilities, not rights. A modern book on marriage might begin by setting out the rights of the wife, and go on – if it was fair – to suggest ways in which the husband should expect to profit from the relationship too. The Bible deliberately sets about things the other way round. First, the wife is reminded of her responsibilities ('Wives, submit to your husbands as to the Lord'); then the husband is reminded of his ('Husbands, love your wives, just as Christ loved the church'). The same balance is struck, but the difference of approach is highly significant. Paul's keynote is service. There is no mention at all of either partner's rights.

Far from treating his wife as a doormat, therefore, a husband who is filling his role as 'head' in the Jesus style will be preoccupied with her growth as a person. As Christ's aim is to see his body, the church, 'built up ... and become mature' (Eph. 4:12–13), so the Christian husband will see to it that his wife's gifts are not stifled but developed to full maturity in marriage. In Paul's body-language, she will be 'fed and cared for' in every way through her husband's loving, serving headship.

Unitive principle

'If a wife loses her submission to her husband, she loses her unity with him,' writes Larry Christenson. 'If a husband abdicates his responsibility as head, he strikes at the very core of the relationship which God has established between him and his wife.'[3]

On the face of it, that sounds a far-fetched claim. Yet there are clear echoes of it in Scripture. Just as it is Christ's aim immediately, in his role as the church's head, to ensure that his body 'grows up' and 'becomes mature', so his ultimate goal is that 'we all reach *unity* in the faith' (Eph. 4:13). In this sense, the language of head and body expresses closeness and inter-dependence. And Paul has no hesitation in drawing the same kind of word picture in his teaching on marriage. 'In the Lord', he writes, to the Christians at Corinth (immediately after explaining again that '... the head of the wife is the husband'), 'woman is not independent of man, nor is man independent of woman. For as woman came from man, so also man is born of woman' (1 Cor. 11:11–12). Perform an amputation at the neck, and both head and body will suffer the same fate.

Back in Ephesians, Paul draws on the creation teaching of Genesis to drive this point home even further. The

[3] L. and N. Christenson, *The Christian Couple* (Kingsway, 1978), pp. 160f.

whole purpose of marriage, he writes, is that 'the two will become one flesh' (5:31; *cf*. Gn. 2:24). The sheer stupidity of a husband abusing his headship is that he injures *himself*. After all, Paul concludes, 'no-one ever hated his own body' (verse 29).

Some modern commentators see an inevitable clash here between the health of a marriage union and the perpetuation of the headship principle within it. How can a healthy relationship possibly survive, they ask, when one partner is always in charge? The Bible's claim is that the principle of headship actually protects and enhances marital unity. So Peter's tail-piece to his instruction, 'Wives ... be submissive to your husbands' is 'Live *in harmony* with one another' (1 Pet. 3:1, 7–8).

Authority and leadership

Doubts have also been raised about the legitimacy of finding the idea of 'authority' in the New Testament's use of the word 'head' when it is applied to the husband's role in marriage. Paul (some suggest) unpacks the meaning of headship in terms of self-sacrificial love and close harmony – but he may not have intended to convey the ideas of authority and leadership as well. Are we reading this extra meaning into his words because we associate the ideas of 'being head' and 'being in charge' so closely today? If so, perhaps John Stuart Mill's vision for 'reciprocal superiority' in marriage comes closer to the New Testament's perspective. He describes this as an arrangement whereby 'each can enjoy the luxury of looking up to the other, and can have alternately the pleasure of leading and being led in the path of development'.

Mill's concept is certainly attractive, but it does not do justice to the whole of the Bible's understanding of headship. It is certainly a vital part of the husband's biblical role as head to see that his wife is free to develop her gifts. He is also to 'look up to her' in the sense of respecting and honouring her as his fellow-heir of eternal life. But that is not quite all that headship involves.

In the Old Testament, as we have seen, the word 'head' can be applied to a family's leader. Paul the Jewish teacher would obviously be familiar with that usage, and in describing the headship of Christ he assumes that his Jewish readers will have no difficulty in linking the ideas of 'head' and 'leader' in their own minds. Jesus, he writes is 'head over everything' (Eph. 1:22). When he goes on, in the same letter, to compare the husband's headship with Christ's, he clearly intends to say (among other things) that the husband should take the lead in married life.

This is confirmed by the expression he uses for the wife's role. The word 'submit' is a strong military term. It implies obedience (*cf.* 1 Pet. 3:1, 6). As twentieth-century western readers of these Bible letters we may wish Paul had hit upon a milder word, but his meaning is uncomfortably clear. A wife who takes the New Testament's teaching on headship seriously must yield to her husband's *authority*, not just to his *needs*.

It is worth noticing, too, that in structuring marriage in this hierarchical fashion Peter and Paul are simply reflecting the way the Bible structures all relationships. Wherever we look in Scripture, the headship principle is built in. Parents are to control their children (Eph. 6:1–3). Masters must be allowed to direct their labour forces (Eph. 6:5–8). Governments have God's authority to rule (Rom. 13:1–7). Man and woman have their Maker's mandate to manage the rest of creation (Gn. 1:28). And even in the perfect relationship of the Godhead, the Father is the Head to whom the Son is subject (1 Cor. 11:3; 15:28). If marriage were *not* hierarchically structured, it would stick out like a sore thumb from every other kind of relationship the Bible describes.

Getting it together

Detaching the idea of authority, then, from those of unity and service, in an effort to grasp the Bible's concept of headship, is as futile as it is unnecessary. Jesus himself served through leadership, just as he led in service. He did not step down from his position of authority when he washed the disciples' feet. He simply exemplified what true leadership meant. 'You call me . . . "Lord",' he said, as he got on with the slave's job, 'and rightly so, for that is what I am' (Jn. 13:13). The same goes for unity as well. Jesus is the Head who 'has the supremacy', and it is only in him as Leader that 'all things hold together' (Col. 1:17–18).

It is in Jesus, too, that the ideas of headship and submission blend perfectly. As 'the head over every power and authority' (Col. 2:10), he sums up all headship. And as the one whom 'God made . . . to be sin for us' (2 Cor. 5:21), he sums up all submission. So if we assume conflict is inevitable in any relationship where one partner is head and the other subordinate, we find ourselves at odds with the way Scripture describes the person and work of Jesus. He was not a one-man civil war.

This, in turn, has important implications for our understanding of what it means to be culturally conditioned. When that phrase is used today, it is often applied to explain away some uncongenial part of the Bible's teaching. Sometimes, too, there is a hidden assumption that our own culture today is superior to anyone else's culture yesterday. The biblical teaching in question is declared no longer relevant because it reflects a less advanced (as well as different) social context than our own.

The Bible's teaching on headship often meets exactly this fate. Because it does not square with our contemporary view of marriage it is labelled 'culturally conditioned' and duly consigned to some dusty shelf in a faraway Museum of Biblical Antiquities, where it can be inspected but not practised. The Bible itself, however, has rather a different slant on cultural conditioning. It warns its readers not to 'conform any longer to the pattern of this world' (Rom. 12:2). In other words, it invites those who take its claim to authority seriously not only to study its message within its own cultural setting, but to judge *their* cultural assumptions by *its* theological truths. If the concept of headship is as heavily backed theologically as I have suggested, it is we who need to adapt to the principle it expresses, not vice versa.

What does this mean in practice? Not, perhaps, quite

what we might assume. The Bible's teaching on headship does not simply provide a back-up for Christian chauvinism. It may, in fact, mean that we need to reassess fairly radically our more conservative views of role-activities and decision-making in marriage. Space does not allow me to spell out the implications at any length, but here are one or two suggestions.

Activities

As far as directing what a man or woman should and should not do in married life, the husband's headship is often taken to mean that he should be the provider and she the home-maker. 'When the Lord appeared to Abraham at Mamre and asked where Sarah was', comments C. Harinck, 'he replied "She is in the tent." That is the special domain of women.'[4]

In fact, the Bible does not draw that conclusion at all. In Genesis 1 God gave both man and woman two *shared* responsibilities. They were to rear children and to manage creation (the latter covering nearly everything we label as work today – Gn. 1:28). The modern, western ideal of the husband commuting to his job while the wife spends her days as a full-time mother and home-maker is a surprisingly recent innovation. As a pattern it is not without its dangers either, especially if 'the job' becomes exclusively the man's preserve and 'the children' the woman's. The Bible tells us that, theologically speaking, it was sin's arrival in Genesis 3 which split parenthood from work. Yet many Christians perpetuate that division today by misquoting the Bible's teaching on headship to support it.

As we have seen, one of the husband's main responsibilities as head is to see that his wife has the freedom to grow as a person and to develop her gifts to their full potential. Seen in this light, the headship principle allows enormous scope for a rich variety of practical expressions.

So far from deterring his wife from going out to work,

[4] C. Harinck, 'The Biblical View of Women in the Church', *The Banner of Truth* 39.5 (May 1973), p. 16.

for example, her Christian 'head' may well take the initiative in persuading her to pursue a career. If family circumstances make it right, he may well find his own niche in the home, working there unpaid while she earns the money. And if that should prove to be the best formula for them both, he will not feel that his ego (or his wife's femininity) is under any threat simply because she, not he, brings home the salary cheque. The biblical structure of headship is not a straitjacket which stops freedom of movement outside narrow, pre-set roles, but the scaffolding round which a marriage relationship can be shaped and grow to maturity.

One result of all this may be that the Christian and the secular feminist will find themselves sharing the same platform on some issues. Their approaches, however, will be very different. By and large, feminism works by competition and confrontation, and takes its stand on a wife's right to make her own independent choices. The principle of headship, by contrast, is more concerned to foster unity and mutual growth, and leaves ultimate decision-making with the husband.

Direction

What, then, of decision-making? Again, we must take care not to apply the Bible's teaching wrongly. Being head does not mean that the husband is under obligation to make and carry through all the decisions of married life. Still less should it mean that he always gets his own way!

Headship in marriage has more to do with establishing its direction than with making lists of decisions. And that, in turn, will involve the fixing of family priorities. In other words, the husband's prime responsibility as head is to keep the marriage on the right course to its goal. That may or may not mean that he will make specific choices and decisions himself (whether or not to take in his elderly mother-in-law, perhaps, or where to go for the family holiday). He will certainly expect his wife to do a lot of the deciding – not because he hasn't the time to attend to details, but because he recognizes that on some important things her judgment is likely to be better than his.

A fine biblical example of this process at work is set out for us in the first chapter of 1 Samuel. Elkanah was about to set off on his annual pilgrimage to the Lord's shrine at Shiloh. He always took his family with him on these occasions, but this time his wife Hannah, who had recently had her first baby, wanted to stay at home. Was she being over-protective towards her young son? Was she making religious excuses to cover up an unhealthy possessiveness? Should she, perhaps, be made to go against her will? Elkanah made up his mind. 'Do what seems best to you,' he told her. She stayed, while he went. Events showed that she was absolutely right – and so was he, as her head.

We are not told whether Elkanah and Hannah had an argument about the right thing to do. Perhaps they did. It is by no means an unhealthy thing when a husband and wife disagree, and the husband who resents his wife voicing (or even having) an opinion of her own has a very twisted view of headship! What matters, of course, is how the differences are resolved. And it is here that some Christians (including some feminist writers) run the risk of talking idealistic nonsense. Certainly it is best to postpone a contested decision whenever possible, to allow time for discussion, prayer, advice and – in the end, we hope – agreement. But supposing the matter in hand is urgent? What if agreement just cannot be reached when the time limit is up? It would be foolish to pretend that such occasions never arise.

The husband's headship is the biblical means for cutting these knots. 'We were operating pretty much independently of each other,' confessed one husband whom Larry and Nordis Christenson introduced to the headship principle. 'She'd make her decisions and I'd make mine, and as long as we didn't get in each other's way things would chug along fairly well. But then we'd both jump in on the same thing, and that's when there'd be fireworks. Now we talk things over a lot more.'[5]

There are few things more hideous than the abuse of

[5] L. and N. Christenson, *The Christian Couple*, p. 132.

headship. But its proper use blends leadership with mutual growth and unity. And that is the Bible's prescription for a happy marriage, modelled on Christ's relationship with his bride, the church.

Response to David Field

Michael Griffiths

I think that David Field has given us a better exposition of the biblical concept of headship than I have read anywhere else. He has expressed it in such a winsome way that many of the worst abuses of the concept would disappear, provided that those who accept what he says about headship accept at the same time the 'delicately tuned' balance that he proposes. (Some threatened husbands may take David's winsome presentation of headship, and to it add a quite unacceptable, dominating face, without care or heart.)

However, there remain some aspects which despite David's protestations still seem to me to be self-contradictory. How can there be absolute equality of status (pp. 45f.), and at the same time hierarchy, which must imply that one party is superior to the other? The comments which follow seem pertinent.

1. *While all three relationships (husband/wife, parent/ child and master/slave) might be described as hierarchical, such a description can obscure the great differences between them.* It is not simply that a wife ought not to be treated as a slave or a child. The master/slave relationship was a temporary social one, which has largely disappeared. The parent/child relationship is a temporary

biological one, in the sense that the aim of the parent is to bring the child to such a level of maturity that it can itself become a parent (indeed, in old age, the roles may in some degree have to be reversed).

It is often overlooked, however, that Christian marriage is also only temporary, 'till death us do part'. In heaven there is neither marriage nor giving in marriage (Mt. 22:30). The unmarried and the married may both be encouraged by recognizing that both are experiencing temporary states, which will be superseded by something better in glory.

2. *Christians are exhorted to be holy like God, and to love as God loves them.* Husbands are exhorted to love their own wives as Christ loved the church. These are exhortations based on comparisons. But that does not mean that, on earth, man is either as holy or as loving as God is. Marriage is only an earthly relationship between fallen, unholy and not always loving human beings. The comparison or parallel is only partial.

3. *The headship of Christ alone is permanent and eternal.* For the purpose of exhorting husbands to love their wives, parallels can be drawn from Christ's loving, sacrificial, considerate, self-giving, initiative-taking headship. But such comparisons illustrate an *attitude*, rather than describe some immutable, permanent difference of hierarchical function between husbands and wives.

4. *A husband's love for his wife is the palest reflection of Christ's love for the church.* Therefore to argue for a concept of headship where the husband carries anything like the absolute authority of Christ over the church is unfortunate. Christ is infallible, impeccable, omniscient, omnipotent and omnipresent. But there are few husbands like this! In relation to Christ, the earthly church is fallible and sinful; full of spots, wrinkles and other such things; its knowledge only part knowledge, its power a derived power.

The comparison of the relationship between husband and wife with that between Christ and his church aptly demonstrates the love of Christ, but it must not be pressed too far. Would it not be totally misleading to suggest, on the basis of that comparison, that the husband is impeccable and infallible, the wife sinful and full of blemishes?

5. *It does not necessarily follow that, because the three relationships proposed above are relevant to the headship of Christ, all three are equally relevant to the headship of husbands to the same extent.* The degree of correspondence varies. The comparison is only a metaphor, used for the purpose of exhortation. It is certainly not absolute, and, as we have seen, it is only of limited duration.

6. *Too great an emphasis on headship and authority obscures the fact that a wife is able, more than anyone else, to rebuke and admonish her husband within the privacy and security of a loving relationship.* Scripture commands mutual admonition (Col. 3:16). What poor fool of a husband has so impoverished a marriage that he learns nothing from his wife?

Richard Baxter, in his *Christian Directory*, says not only that a husband is the chief instrument in his wife's sanctification (in several senses!), but also that a wife is the chief instrument in her husband's (and, too, not merely in a passive sense!). Pressing the idea of headship to the extreme of 'authority' (the Bible never uses that word about husband/wife relationships, except in a mutual sense), may thus prevent the husband from making that progress in sanctification to which his wife can help him, just as, reciprocally, he can help her.

My difficulty, then, is that in spite of the gracious protestations to the contrary, we are still presented with too hierarchical and authoritarian a structure, which becomes dangerous if used by a weak and threatened husband to bolster up his position.

Headship must mean in the Ephesian context that the husband takes a lead in loving, and takes the initiative to sacrifice himself for the sake of his wife (Eph. 5:25). It is presented in the context of a mutual submission 'to one another' (Eph. 5:21), indeed, within the same sentence, where the word 'authority' is not used at all.

In order to attach it to the comparison of the headship of Christ to that of the husband, the 'head over everything' phrase has to be dragged roughshod out of its context (Eph. 1:22), through four whole chapters. This seems arbitrary – and unnecessary! The aspect of headship used in the context is an attractive one. Why spoil it by introducing aspects foreign to the context, which fail to recognize the incompleteness of the comparison?

Response to Elizabeth Catherwood

Valerie Griffiths

Elizabeth Catherwood has given us a necessary reminder that two people cannot commit themselves to the closest of all lifelong relationships and still function independently. They must carefully work out how they can function together.

However, I would question whether a woman's total life can be defined in terms of 'a primary concern to help her husband', or that she was 'made by God to help man to function as God's representative in this world'. Such statements leave single women without a role. It would seem to be far more in accordance with Scripture to say that women were made by God to function *with* men as God's representatives.

Historically, women have always worked alongside their husbands to survive, and this has involved heavy physical work such as farming, housework, and carrying water. By the time she stopped bearing children in her forties, a woman was old and had few years left. It was only in the last century that a leisured middle class evolved, in which wives stayed at home while servants cared for their house and men worked elsewhere. Even without servants, such a lifestyle may eventually be seen to have been a temporary western luxury. Nevertheless Elizabeth has rightly stressed the housewife's enormous privilege of

68

flexibility of time, and her responsibility to use it rightly before the Lord.

I would also question the 'different roles for men and women laid down by God in the beginning'. Certainly, biology has until very recently dictated that the birth and care of children will define much of most adult women's lives. But at the same time, woman has an existence apart from her children, and there are examples in Scripture of women called by the Lord to other tasks. Deborah the wife of Lappidoth (to whom Elizabeth herself refers) also served as prophet and judge; the people of Israel would go to her for decisions (Jdg. 4:5). She called Barak to organize resistance against Sisera and go to battle. Huldah wife of Shallum was a prophetess, called upon for an authoritative decision on the value of the book found in the temple (there were several men who could have been consulted instead). The lady of Proverbs 31 was a business woman, who ran a home industry and staff so efficiently that her husband could trust her and leave her to act, even in the buying of property.

In the New Testament, Martha was rebuked for her 'womanly' preoccupation with feeding a dozen or more guests. Mary was commended for taking her place as a disciple at the feet of the Rabbi – a position allowed only to men. In Jewish law women were not accepted as witnesses; yet the Lord chose them to take the greatest message of all, the news of the resurrection, to his disciples.

Far too many books on 'Women in the Bible' wrongly read modern evangelical ideals into these lives. In fact there are many instances where women did 'men's' work, and now that families are smaller and people live longer, it is becoming increasingly evident that in many areas women and men can do the same work equally well. Many concepts of men's and women's work owe more to tradition than to any innate characteristics of either sex. This is not to deny the differences between men and women; but as Christians we have so stressed the different roles that we have failed to find adequate expression for the common humanity equally shared by man and woman.

Society around us is tackling this today; it is time that Christians faced it too.

I agree with Elizabeth that families of Christian workers need to think through their priorities very carefully. But I do not think that in such a brief treatment it is helpful to raise the enormous questions associated with missionaries' children. Each family's circumstances differ so widely that only the parents and mission leaders on the spot can make the right decisions before the Lord. Few do it without enormous heart-searching and prayer, and the situation can change from year to year. Parents separated from their children are particularly vulnerable to spiritual attack, and I have already seen the grief and agony caused to missionaries overseas by well-meaning but ignorant correspondence in Christian magazines here. If Christians want to help, they must first listen, and understand the problems involved. Then they must see that each family has adequate finance to do what it believes to be right before God in its own circumstances. One of the most positive contributions towards solving the problem in recent years has been the generosity of Christians who have made it possible for so many children to visit their parents overseas at least once a year.

In conclusion, I wish that David Field and Elizabeth Catherwood could be more specific on the subject of what headship and decision-making actually involve for them. Many people claim to function on the principle that the husband makes final decisions, and yet, when pressed, they admit that actually they talk things through and come to decisions together. There is a grave danger of advocating one thing and doing another. In happy marriages, based on mutual respect for each other's gifts, there is rarely a problem. But where headship is abused, there is grave danger. A recent article in a Christian magazine assured a rather 'weak' young man that 'a girl wants someone who deserves all her love, loyalty and devotion'. True. How else can a woman respect her husband? But it went on to add, '... someone who isn't afraid to say "No" sometimes, even when it cuts across her wishes'.

We all have to face this at times. But to encourage some

people to assert their masculinity by cutting across other people's wishes is scarcely Christian, and is a recipe for disaster. However, where the wife respects her husband, where the husband honours his wife, where each in humility counts the other better than themselves, there is a basis for respect, mutual consultation, love and unity.

Mankind: male and female

Valerie Griffiths

The creation of mankind · Mankind in identity and diversity · Broken relationships · Identity and diversity in the twentieth century · Facing change · Relating in marriage · The dangers of stereotypes · Changing life-cycles · Functioning together · A glance backwards · New paths overseas · The way ahead

Every generation must go back to basic biblical principles and then discover how they are to be followed and applied in a new time and a new culture. With this purpose in mind we will begin by re-examining the creation of mankind (Gn. 1 – 2), and then consider the effect of mankind's disobedience and fall (Gn. 3). Then we will consider the light shed on these principles by the social sciences, and consider how this affects men and women both in marriage and in society. Since all knowledge and truth comes from the Creator himself, it is important that we should be aware of modern insights and understanding where these are in accordance with the Word of God, and that we should use them to help us to apply his Word to our lives today.

At the same time, we must recognize, as Dorothy Pape[1] has shown, how much our cultural prejudices, presuppositions and sheer spiritual blindness have controlled not only our exposition of God's Word, but even our translation of it.

---

[1] D. Pape, *God and Woman* (Mowbrays, 1978).

The creation of mankind

Genesis 1 states very simply, 'Then God said, "Let us make man in our image, after our likeness; and let them have dominion . . . over all the earth. . . ." So God created man in his own image, in the image of God he created him; male and female he created them . . . and God saw everything that he had made, and behold, it was very good' (Gn. 1:26–31).

The first word 'man' carries the sense of 'mankind' in Hebrew. Mankind was created in duality, male and female, and together they constitute mankind, and together reflect the image of God, and together exercise dominion over the earth. Argument has raged in the past over the meaning of 'image and likeness'. Since God is spirit, the description cannot refer to physical likeness; and it is something which distinguishes man from animals. Even the words 'let us make' distinguish the creation of mankind from the rest of creation. It *does* indicate that if mankind is made in God's image, then God is not 'wholly other', different, alien, incomprehensible to man. There can be a meaningful intelligible relationship between God and man. In so far as mankind is given specific commands – 'Thou shalt not' – it also suggests moral, rational, autonomous beings who can be held responsible for their actions. The immediate context further suggests that the lordship mankind was to exercise over creation also stemmed from the image of God which they both bore, and the plural pronoun used by God 'in our image' suggests, in retrospect, the fellowship of the three Persons in one Godhead. This should be reflected by male and female (as they constitute mankind) in relationship with God and with each other. Whatever is said about mankind applies equally to both man and woman. There is no distinction.

Mankind in identity and diversity

In the second chapter of Genesis we are given further details of the act of creation; and, for the first time, God decrees that something in his creation is *not* good. David Clines comments:

> In Genesis 1 the 'good' is what comes perfected from the hand of God, 'good' is his judgment on his own work. . . . An isolated man without others of his own kind is therefore a blot on creation, the one 'no good' part of a perfect world. One man is no man. God cannot pronounce the creation of Adam good until Eve also is made.[2]

The man is alone, and none of his kind can be found in the animal kingdom. While he sleeps, the Creator makes a woman from his side, to be a 'helper fit for him', and the man, on waking, cries out, 'She shall be called Woman (Hebrew: *ishshah*) because she was taken out of Man (*ish*).'

Four facts have led people to assume from these passages the secondary and even inferior status of woman in relation to man, although there is no explicit statement on subordination in this passage: firstly, she was created after the man in time; secondly, she was 'taken' from him; thirdly, she was named by him; and fourthly, she was created as his 'helper'.

We need to consider these briefly. In the first place, priority in time does not necessarily indicate hierarchy and superiority. The animals are created prior to man in Genesis 1 and the man is created prior to woman in Genesis 2. Man himself is created from the dust.

Secondly, the woman was 'taken' from the man – but the man was formed from dust already created, and his creation glorifies the Creator, not the dust. When woman was formed man was totally passive, asleep. God's direct purposeful act brought her into being. The method emphasizes the common humanity which they share.

Thirdly, with regard to the naming, in Genesis 2:23 the man cries 'she shall be called Woman (*ishshah*)'; and the words he uses differ from those used for naming the

[2] D. J. Clines, 'A Biblical Doctrine of Man' (Christian Brethren Research Fellowship No. 28, 1976), p. 33.

animals in verse 20. It sounds like the female form of *ish*, 'man', but is in fact, different and probably comes from *anash*, 'mankind'. It is not a personal name. After the survey of all the animal creation and the failure to find one of his own kind, here at last is his true counterpart, drawn from his very self and like him. Here was no animal but another human being. McNally translates it 'This is me!' and the cry expressed their common nature and identity, someone as human as himself, the true companion and counterpart in God's plan.

Dorothy Pape comments,

> They originated from one flesh, were separated into male and female and in the divine provision of marriage would again become one flesh. There is nothing about the man ruling over the woman, only that he leave his parents and cleave to his wife; together they would form a new independent unit.[3]

Fourthly, we come to the phrase 'a helper fit for [corresponding to] him'. Calvin interpreted this as meaning that a woman was 'a kind of appendage to the man', owing her existence entirely to the necessity for supplying his needs. Clyde Narramore says, 'Woman was not made for herself, but to complete the man.'[4] This is another instance where the culture of the commentator prejudges the interpretation. The Hebrew word 'helper' occurs twenty-one times in the Old Testament. Apart from its use twice here of the woman, four of these occurrences are general usages and the other fifteen are references to God as the 'helper' of his people; so it cannot in itself mean that the 'helper' is secondary and subordinate to the one helped.

So far the only 'rule' mentioned is that of mankind over creation – not over each other. In their own relationship, mutual need and complementarity are clear. They are created to serve God together. Man on his own is not

---

[3] J. McNally, *The Place of Woman in the N.T. Church* (Unpublished Master's Thesis, Wheaton, 1944), quoted in D. Pape, *God and Woman*, pp. 156f.

[4] C. Narramore, *A Woman's World* (Grand Rapids, Michigan, 1963), quoted in D. Pape, *God and Woman*, p. 165.

self-sufficient. There are areas where he is lacking. When woman was created she was endowed with those gifts which complemented and completed his, in order to provide the 'wholeness' of mankind. As D. J. Clines puts it,

> What Adam lacks, therefore, is not so much a wife so that he may procreate like all the animals, but another person so that he may become a human being. The similarity of the two sexes is more important than the difference.[5]

Marlene Cohen adds, 'It is not only in marriage that God has joined male and female together; they are together in his basic purposes for the human race.'[6]

Broken relationships

When we move on to Genesis 3, we find the perfect relationship of the man and the woman, with each other and with God, shattered. They were not created to be puppets – they were given the dignity to choose, to respond of their own will to their Creator; and they chose to disobey. The disobedience broke their relationship with God, with each other and with creation. In consequence they were excluded from the garden, the place of fellowship with God, and God said their own relationship would be characterized by rule and servitude, childbirth would be associated with pain for the woman, and daily survival would involve hard labour for the man. For the first time the rule of one person over another is mentioned. H. Thielicke comments, 'the correspondence of dominion and servitude is the very mark of the disturbance caused by the fall.'[7]

The Lord may be pronouncing judgment on the couple for their sin, or simply describing the outworking of sin

---

[5] D. J. Clines, 'A Biblical Doctrine of Man', p. 33.

[6] M. Cohen, 'Agenda for a Biblical Church' (*National Evangelical Anglican Congress Report*, Anglican Information Office, Sydney, 1981), Vol. 1, p. 146.

[7] H. Thielicke, *The Ethics of Sex* (Allen and Unwin, 1964), p. 13.

in their lives. If it is the former, then the consequences of sin have been dealt with for ever at the cross, and we must learn to live as those redeemed by Christ and no longer under condemnation (Rom. 12:1). If it is the latter, then such consequences can no longer be accepted with resignation but challenged in the name of Christ. To support the continuation of such a broken relationship is to continue in sin. The gospel of Jesus Christ brings reconciliation between God and mankind and the restoration of a broken relationship both now and in a more complete way in the future. It does no less in reconciling male and female, and restoring to them the positive complementarity of partnership God intended from the beginning, and such a reconciliation and partnership should be demonstrated to the world here and now. True, sin remains – but only as something to be overcome through the power of Christ working within us.

A study of the Gospels, Acts and the epistles provides much evidence that the early church was beginning to face these implications and put them into practice. Marlene Cohen comments:

> No aspects of the fall of man and of the consequences of that fall were in the *purposes* of God. . . . His purpose before and after the fall is that men and women should still bear his image (through the work of Christ on the cross) and still exercise proper dominion over the earth.[8]

Identity and diversity in the twentieth century

Adam and Eve could rejoice in each other before the fall, in the wonder of their shared humanity, their identity, their unity, and also the variety and complementarity sparked off by their differences as male and female. Both the identity and the variety are God-given.

The challenge today is to discover what it means in the twentieth century for men and women to relate to each other, both in their identical humanity and in their sexual

[8] M. Cohen, *NEAC Report*, Vol. 1, p. 144.

differentiation, and together to have dominion over the earth. The basic principles have not changed.

In this century, women have been moving back into society, functioning alongside men and very often doing the same work, as fellow human beings. Sometimes people are so concerned to stress the differences between male and female that they overlook their identity in humanity. The Women's Liberation movement, of course, stresses the identity, and totally denies the sexual differentiation found in Scripture. Most Christians have no problem accepting the common humanity and the sexual differentiation. The problem today lies in the relationship between the two areas. Does the sexual differentiation demand totally different functions for men and women throughout their lives? Or does the common humanity mean that, apart from the differences dictated by biology in childbearing and child-raising, men and women can tackle the same work, as human beings, bringing to that work their own masculine and feminine gifts?

As male and female they are created different in every cell of their bodies. This is demonstrated most clearly in their biological relationship, but goes even further; yet the non-anatomical differences are extraordinarily elusive to demonstrate and define. Masculinity is popularly identified with being physically strong, tough, independent, rational, objective, unemotional, efficient, competitive, aggressive. Yet immediately we can think of many men who are notably gentle, sensitive and caring. Femininity is commonly associated with being physically weaker, dependent, subjective, sensitive, emotional, passive, modest, quiet, gentle. Yet many (the majority?) are not. Indeed motherhood requires physical strength, endurance, resilience, patience, independence, decision-making, organization, firmness and understanding – to name but a few qualities.

The fact is that the male/female characteristics form a spectrum which varies in each individual. There are certain 'masculine' and 'feminine' traits at each end of the spectrum – the tough, aggressive, strong at one end, and gentle, passive, dependent at the other. But the vast majority of people fall in the centre where male and female characteristics overlap. Some men are gentler, some women are tougher, and the popular stereotypes of male and female often have far more to do with cultural stereotypes (and even fantasies), than innate biology or biblical decree.

S. B. Clark, in a massive work which examines the roles of men and women in the Bible and in the social sciences, comments:

> The most significant differences between men and women lie in their psychological structure and social behaviour rather than in intelligence, skill and behaviour.... A woman's emotions, intellect and body form a more integrated unity than those of a man. She confronts decisions, activities, relationships as an entire person – a blend of emotions, intellect and body. On the other hand, a man's emotions, intellect and body are more differentiated. He more easily compartmentalizes elements of his personality, treating them as aspects of his identity which he can at times temporarily ignore.[9]

The important thing to note here is that neither is good or bad. Man and woman are created by God, to function together; and each needs to be counterbalanced by the other.

Facing change

Throughout history the biological difference has inevitably dictated the major difference in function between the two. Until this century a woman's adult life was filled with the bearing and upbringing of children, and therefore her role as wife and mother took priority over everything else she did. A man's role as husband and father required him to provide for the family and in the last two centuries this has meant spending most of the day outside the home in society. Once a couple were married their roles were

[9] S. B. Clark, *Man and Woman in Christ* (Servant Books, 1980), pp. 377, 381.

defined, and freedom of choice was limited.

Today the mother's role no longer defines the whole of her adult life. Firstly, many women remain single. Secondly, with smaller families motherhood occupies less than half a woman's adult working life. Motherhood is no longer the only goal for girls, and the State has taken over such responsibilities as education and health care – traditional areas of work for mothers. Instead of lamenting changing family patterns it is time Christians rethought the issues involved, and welcomed the new opportunities ahead.

Relating in marriage

Modern couples may not find it easy to face the changes, and it is all too easy to forget that the marriage relationship is still vulnerable as a result of the fall, and sin can very easily creep in to destroy the relationship God intended. Paul Tournier describes the day when his wife quietly commented 'You are my doctor, my psychologist, even my pastor; but you are not my husband.'[10] He was dumbfounded, but it led to a great deal of heart-searching in the years that followed. He was deeply attached to his wife, and with his education and psychiatric training had done all he could to draw her out of her diffidence and reticence. He had been greatly concerned to help her, but from an unconscious position of superiority, and she perceived it long before he did. He writes: 'It was not until we came together in God's presence and I confessed my own feelings, that she felt that *I* needed her help as much as she needed mine, and that I had as much to learn from her as she from me. That is real equality.'[11] He needed far more than a homemaker and housekeeper. He had buried personal feelings under intellectual objectivity, and he desperately needed his wife to help him to become a whole person. After a lifetime in medical practice he reluctantly commented, 'I think there is in men's hearts an uncon-

[10] P. Tournier, *The Gift of Feeling* (SCM Press, 1981), p. 102.
[11] *Ibid.*, p. 110.

scious contempt for women . . .'

Marriage should be an exercise in true mutuality and partnership, where neither dominates the other – to do so is to diminish and depersonalize one of God's children. Both share and contribute the gifts God has given to them, and both learn from each other before the Lord. It is here that our cultural interpretation of the husband as 'decision-maker' can break down. John Wilson, expounding Ephesians 5:21 – 6:9, comments:

> Headship does not sanctify masculine desires to dominate as though it is the male prerogative to exercise power over others, as though the male is to subdue and the female is to be subdued.[12]

Marlene Cohen asks how many Christian husbands and wives actually reach the point of deadlock, or should in fact reach it. In a healthy relationship most couples discuss decisions together, and where there is disagreement, they can agree to compromise. Marlene Cohen adds:

> As each partner has expertise . . . any headship of man is correctly exercised by a decision to make use of that experience, not by a decision to over-ride it.[13]

To make decisions which over-ride the views of wife and children devalues them as people and leads to broken relationships. Marriage is a relationship of trust where both partners commit themselves totally to the other, believing that the other will not abuse such trust. R. K. Johnston comments:

> The reference to wives being subject to their husbands (Eph. 5:22–24) can be adequately understood only in terms of the subjection commanded in verse 21, the sacrificial love of the husband prescribed in verses 25–30 and the unity of the marriage partners in verses 31–33.[14]

Marlene Cohen adds:

[12] *NEAC Report*, Vol. 2, p. 153.   [13] *Ibid.*, Vol. 1, p. 154.
[14] R. K. Johnston, *Evangelicals at an impasse* (John Knox Press, Atlanta), p. 69.

As Christ first gave himself, so husbands are to first give themselves. The church is to respond to Christ in self-giving: wives are to give themselves in response to their husbands . . . Jesus Christ is man's model for headship. Any self assertion (male or female) that seeks its own rights at the expense of others cannot be condoned.[15]

The dangers of stereotypes

The relationship of men and women within the home is usually described in terms of fixed roles – a concept that is convenient, but dangerous and unbiblical. It is dangerous because it begins with the role and demands that the individuals adjust, regardless of their gifts. Square pegs are failures if they won't go into round holes, and those who can't conform to the system are criticized for failure. But this is to reject people as God has made them in their infinite variety. There is never one stereotype for a Christian home. Each couple, according to their gifts, strengths and weaknesses, must come together to do God's will.

There is widespread concern about the stress on homes today, but much is aggravated by clinging to old cultural patterns. The industrial revolution, the separation of home from a man's place of work, and the size of the modern nuclear family, all serve to isolate mothers at home. Cut off from the stimulus and variety of society, they spend their time with other mothers and children. Tournier describes it as 'off-stage, exiled from the reality of life'.[16] They are better educated and trained than ever before in history, and when they get depressed and restless with hours of routine housework, they are accused of 'failing to accept their biblical role'. Betty Friedan describes their problem as 'mindlessness'.[17] Most men, if called to spend their whole lives as husbands and fathers, on the garden, decorating, car-washing, *etc.* would also have problems.

15 *NEAC Report*, Vol. 1, pp. 152–153.
16 Tournier, *op. cit.*, p. 40.
17 B. Friedan, *The Feminine Mystique* (W. W. Norton, 1963).

The very people who assure a mother of the value of her work usually have no desire to do it themselves. However vital it is for the family, it is considered 'woman's work', and demeaning for a man. Today, as men get busier and busier, more and more routine chores devolve on the wife – even heavy gardening, car-washing and decorating. In fact a great deal of the routine work in a home has nothing to do with sexual gifts and differences – it can be done by either partner equally well. What is dull for one is probably dull for both! But if a growing family, starting with the father, learn to work as a team and share the chores, a great deal will be lifted from the mother who will then have time and strength to use her special gifts where they are needed most.

There is a further danger in resorting to roles. If a woman's role as wife and mother in the home is stressed too much, the father's role becomes minimal. The pressure of the secular world may make a father the financial provider, but a visitor in his own home, 'cut off, absorbed in himself, with little interest in the children's lives'.[18] He may well help when children are small, but then withdraw under increasing pressures at work. Teenage boys in such families grow up without any male pattern in the home. Father's work is 'outside'. Home is where he crashes out. It is scarcely surprising if they then fail to relate to their own wives and families and homes break up. Mothers are not blameless either. Helen Franks comments that many are possessive of their own territory; after all, they have no other. They make their children, instead of their husbands, the centre of their lives. They thrive on the love they extract from the children, and load the authority on to the father, until the children mature and leave home and a lonely man and woman are left with nothing in common.

Most people fear change. The world today needs men and women who can tackle the current social changes in a creative and constructive way together. There are radicals whose experience as children and adults has so embittered

---

[18] Helen Franks, *Prime Time* (Pan, 1981), pp. 36–37.

them that they call for the end of marriage and family, and look instead to communities. They are few in number. Many of the communal experiments which have been tried, have failed. There are others whose marriages have failed for one reason or another who still look back to the family as the ideal, in spite of current pressures tearing it apart. Mary Kenny,[19] interviewing a wide variety of women about their homes and careers, found that the majority put their homes and children first, and a financially independent wife did not usually destroy the marriage relationship. Instead they were more dependent on their husbands than housebound mothers and freely acknowledged this. They could not combine home and career without their husband's support.

Changing life-cycles

Gail Sheehy[20] has investigated changing patterns for women in America. She has identified five. Firstly, the caregivers in society who happily pour out their lives in serving not only their families but society too. When their children are older these people reach out to the needy around. Modern society is increasingly in need of people with such gifts. Secondly, there are those who hope for marriage and a career. Some may opt for marriage and family first and pick up a career when the children are in their teens; others will put their career first and hope to marry and have children later. Thirdly, the 'integrators' try to combine marriage, career and motherhood in their twenties. 'It is rarely possible, and it is time some of us who have tried it said so. Most integrators subtracted the marriage, or gave up on the career or the children.' Fourthly, there are those who choose to stay single (and they may also be caregivers). Finally there are the transients, who can settle nowhere. If girls are to face the realities of today they will aim not only at marriage but at some

[19] Mary Kenny, *Women X Two: How to Cope with a Double Life* (Hamlyn, 1979), pp. 37, 47.
[20] Gail Sheehy, *Passages: Predictable Crises of Adult Life* (Corgi, 1977), pp. 295–296.

proper training and experience for adult life, so that when the years of mothering have passed they can tackle the second half of adult life in a positive way.

Increasing numbers of couples are moving in this direction. There are, of course, numerous problems and tensions which arise, and the changes demand maturity and co-operation from both husband and wife. But I would suggest that it is a positive Christian approach for the changing world of today. In Luke 11:27 Jesus directs attention away from woman's child-bearing function, to the fundamental prerequisite of obeying God. Yet many Christian books on the family almost idolize the home. Certainly the woman should fulfil her responsibility as mother when she is most needed. But as the children grow up, she should use her years of acquired experience and her particular gifts and training to face major changes beyond the home, either in voluntary work (which is increasingly needed in today's society) or in paid work.

I say 'should', because all Christians should be seeking God's will at each stage of their lives, and all are responsible for what they do with the time he gives them. Jesus specifically told all Christian disciples not to spend all their time on food, drink and clothing (Mt. 6:25–33). At the same time, others must not force the matter. The couple will need to seek the Lord's will for the wife, and the husband will need to face any adjustments demanded of him; but the result can enrich both of them. This is a far cry from the wife who is urged to 'leave all the decisions to her husband'; but Eve was not created to cater for Adam's material needs, or produce his children. She was to be a 'helper corresponding to him', with a wider responsibility in creation. Too many wives stagnate at home without the stimulus of public life, and are finally unable to meet their husband's need for companionship. They are no longer 'helpers' fit for him. As E. Achtemeier expresses it:

> It is doubtful, in fact, that any secular view of liberation can adequately free either male or female from his or her traditional marital role in our society. It takes a new view of society, to be sure, but a vision

that rises out of a conviction about our ultimate responsibility to God for the full exercise of our personalities.... Christian husbands should ... affirm the full implications and freedom given to females in the Christian faith. Indeed it is Christian husbands who should uncompromisingly refuse to allow their wives to exercise anything less than full talents of heart, soul, mind and strength which God has given them. Wives should be encouraged by their husbands to educate and use their minds and to perform to the full extent of their abilities. Husbands should see to it that roles in the home are adjusted in such a way that full growth and exercise of personality are made possible for their mates. Otherwise husbands are not living out the Christian gospel and they are not following the second great commandment by loving their wives as they love themselves.[21]

When we turn to contemporary society, we find once more a situation of increasingly rapid change – change which is steadily ending some of the most basic structures of life itself. As the pace of life increases, people come under increasing tension, and personal relationships, marriage, family, *etc.* all begin to fragment. It is a strange irony that with more people and better communications we are still being depersonalized.

Functioning together

Paul Tournier suggests that:

The loss of a sense of person in our modern civilisation coincided with the seclusion of women into the intimacy of the home and their exclusion from political, economic and cultural life.[22]

Tournier talks of two complementary poles: 'the taste for things and the sense of the person, between which a just

[21] E. Achtemeier, *The Committed Marriage* (Westminster Press, Philadelphia, 1976), pp. 89–90.
[22] P. Tournier, *The Gift of Feeling*, p. 15.

balance must be re-established in our civilisation. They
more or less correspond to the complementarity between
man and woman . . .' He recognizes that this is not absolute: 'There are men who have this sense of the person, and
women whose bent is toward technology and things'.[23] As
society became more complex, the 'masculine' traits of
power, aggression, reason, objectivity and efficiency
predominated, with their emphasis on science and technology. These have come to be admired in society as good
and strong. By contrast the 'feminine' traits of emotion,
sensitivity, tenderness, kindness, respect for others and
concern for personal relationships, though appreciated in
the home, have been devalued in society at large and
labelled as weak. Tournier sums up the Western world as:

> advanced, powerful, efficient, but cold, hard, and
> tedious; a world in which diseases accessible to objec-
> tive study are vanquished, but in which neuroses
> related to lack of love are multiplied, in which we
> have amassed a great wealth of things, while the
> quality of life has deteriorated.[24]

'Men can put a man on the moon', comments Ariana
Stassinopoulos, 'but how well can they handle the relational problems on earth?'[25] Jean Baker Miller makes the
same point.[26] Women are most conscious of 'feelings of
vulnerability, weakness, helplessness, dependency and the
basic emotional connections between an individual and
other people'. Again these things have been dismissed by
society as 'weak', but there is a growing realization in
psychology that these attributes are fundamental to the
quality of human experience, and are in fact 'strengths'.
Paul Tournier pleads for women with their sense of
relationship to exercise these strengths outside the home
today, to counteract the dehumanized state into which
society is rapidly slipping. It is ironical that in this century
some women are fighting to prove that it is only their

[23] *Ibid.*, p. 13.   [24] *Ibid.*, p. 23.
[25] A. Stassinopoulos, *The Female Woman* (Fontana, 1974), p. 106.
[26] Jean Baker Miller, *Toward a New Psychology of Women* (Penguin, 1978), p. 23.

cultural upbringing which differentiates them from men. The truth is that dominion over the earth by either sex alone is bound to be defective. They were created to function together.

A glance backwards

It is significant that the biblical principles of identity in humanity and differentiation in sex have been reflected in the overall development of the women's movement in the last 200 years. In a thought-provoking analysis of the feminist movement from 1840 to 1970, O. Banks[27] has identified three important influences. The first was evangelical Christianity. With the growing influence on personal religious commitment and responsibility, many early-nineteenth-century Christians, both men and women, became concerned over the immorality and double standards in society and the threat these posed to family life, the prevalence of drunkenness, and the exploitation of poorer women and children. They called for protective legislation and minimum wages, and increased welfare for women and children. They were affirming the traditional role of women in the home, recognizing the essential differences between male and female, and trying to protect women in the areas where they were particularly vulnerable – at home and in society. They worked not only for their own rights, but for the poor who had no influence or protection at all. Their Christian concern for human beings did much to change the conditions and quality of life in nineteenth-century England. Christian teaching today still tends to focus on the differences between the sexes.

The second element emerged from the Enlightenment tradition with its emphasis on reason, natural law and the equal rights of every human being, all concepts which lay behind the French Revolution. They were so concerned to affirm the equality of male and female that they virtually denied the innate differences between them and stressed the common humanity of all, and the importance of

[27] O. Banks, *Faces of Feminism* (Robertson, 1981), pp. 7–8.

environment and education in developing people as human beings. Most Christians today have not yet faced up to the implications of this for relationships between men and women in home, society and church life.

The third movement was much more radical, and could only envisage women becoming freed from traditional roles if communities replaced families in caring for children. The experiments in this direction did not succeed for long. The modern Women's Liberation movement has affinities with the last two groups but also displays marked divergences.

The first two groups are most relevant for us, but have often found themselves in conflict, the one stressing women's special role and function and vulnerability, the other their common humanity with men. Biblically, both the differences and the identity are God-given, and both must be exercised responsibly. To confine married women entirely to the role of wife and mother is to deny them the wider contribution God calls them to fulfil as human beings in society. To deny them their special function as women in marriage and motherhood also deprives them of a God-given calling. In the past marriage and motherhood have shaped the whole of their adult lives. Today they need not, and we must ensure that older women are free to fulfil their God-given responsibility beyond the home.

Most people now associate early feminism with women's suffrage. In fact the right to vote was more of an afterthought and unimportant for many. Women were driven to seek it because they found that, as they tackled moral and economic oppression, their greatest opponents were those with commercial and political power who should have acted on their behalf. The women themselves were powerless, and could do nothing to put right the evils which abounded. Jean Baker Miller[28] distinguishes between power for oneself and power to influence others for their good. The one is selfish, the other good. If women are to 'exercise dominion in the world' and make their

[28] J. Baker Miller, *op. cit.*, p. 121.

contribution in society, they must be given the freedom and status to put it into effect. Too often in the past, when women have raised questions that reflect this responsibility, the issues have been pushed aside and labelled as trivial by those who make the decisions. In fact the issues are often far from trivial. To claim that women are unfit by nature for leadership and influence is to deny their calling at creation and the common humanity which they share equally with men. The gift of leadership is not a matter of being male or female, but of a gift received from a sovereign Creator. If they are always kept in a subordinate position, it is hard for women to make an effective contribution. It is like locking someone in a room and leaving them 'free' to act, read, think or suggest. If all they produce is then filtered through the evaluation of others who fail to discern its significance and reject it, their 'freedom' becomes meaningless and frustrating. There is a place for men and women to meet with their own sex, but normally, unless both contribute, something is lacking in the way mankind functions.

At the same time, we do not live only as male and female. In many areas of society today men and women are equally effective as human beings in the jobs they do, and both must be given equal opportunities to serve in society. Married women may need special help because of their dual responsibility to home and work, but they have much to offer to society after years of bringing up a family, if they are given the opportunity and the further training which is often necessary. A married school nurse certainly may not need the money she earns, but finds her job goes far beyond day-to-day mishaps in a day school. She finds herself drawn into bereavement situations and all kinds of family problems. In her mature years she has much to offer as a Christian working in a broken society.

As manufacturing becomes mechanized, the expanding work area of society will be the service section – people – where the key skill required is the ability to relate to other people and to interact with them and care for them. This is where many women's gifts lie, and today's world is waiting for them.

New paths overseas

The secular world is already beginning to grapple with the question of a woman's place in marriage and society, both as a woman and as a human being. Sadly, the churches lag far behind, and an almost pathological fear of change seems to underlie many people's thinking. It may help to look briefly at Christian work overseas for some form of comparison. Anybody accustomed to the greater freedom and participation enjoyed by women serving overseas is, on returning to this country, struck by the very limited avenues of Christian service available to women here. Striking, too, are the formidable numbers of Christian men who dominate the Christian scene. It is so much a part of our Christian tradition that we scarcely notice it.

When Hudson Taylor faced the enormous task of reaching the 400,000,000 people in inland China, he knew from experience that if the church is to minister to a world of men and women, both men and women must be sent. It is hard for us to realize how radical a step he took when, only ten years after Florence Nightingale returned from the Crimea, he set sail in 1865 with his own family, five single men and nine single women. At that time some missionary societies were affirming that the place of wives and fiancées was 'in the home'. The way ahead was uncharted; but, under the guidance of God, he took that first step. Others would follow.

Today missionary societies have changed; but most churches have not. It is much easier to allow our innate conservatism to control us and to go on as we are, than to face something new and different, the implications of which are unknown. But if we are truly sensitive to the continuing presence of sin in male/female relationships, we shall work for change.

The early church, under the guidance of the Holy Spirit, moved forward with power and courage. It was truly a new society, a vivid contrast to normal society around it. The church communities present a picture of sharing and fellowship between men and women. Paul can write to a church he has never visited, and greet no less than nine

91

women personally, referring to some as fellow-workers, colleagues. How many church leaders could do the same today?[29] The radical transformation of attitudes can have come only from Jesus' own ministry, where hierarchy is condemned (Mt. 20:25–28) and the emphasis is upon humbly serving each other. The task of the early church demanded the active participation of all, both men and women. In their responsibility as mothers, women were less free to travel than men at that time, but they worked alongside them as partners and colleagues wherever they could.

By contrast the church today has a morbid fear of change, of what might happen if women exercised a fuller spiritual ministry in the church, and almost no-one has experience in this – except on the mission field. It is therefore relevant to ask, what happens when men and women go overseas?

Firstly, an examination of Protestant denominational and interdenominational societies in Britain shows that in the majority of these societies between 60% and 70% of the members are women. That is a remarkably consistent proportion. Many reasons have been suggested for the 'lack' of men – their commitment to the home ministry, or their family responsibilities, *etc*. Perhaps we need to face the simple fact that for every man he sends overseas, the Lord may choose to call two women. If our traditional home structures are so rigid that women do not have freedom to serve the Lord fully within them, is the Lord using women overseas in order to shake the home churches out of their ruts?

Secondly, how absolute are the roles of men and women? Do men follow the 'masculine' roles and women

[29] Traditionally women's work has been run by women, and today a small church of 100 members may have half a dozen women's groups functioning. They develop their own leadership and speakers and can be the most effective section in church outreach, and yet an overseas couple who recently investigated the approach and methods of various churches in the UK, found the women's activities were rarely mentioned. For some reason they didn't 'count' with the church leaders. It is rare for the women leaders to be offered any practical help and training for the work they do.

the traditional 'feminine' – supportive, dependent – ones? As opportunities permit, the leaders and individuals concerned seek to discover the spiritual gifts given to each member, and to find a niche in which they can fulfil their calling. In contrast with some church structures, it is extraordinarily simple.

And when people are given the freedom to serve as God leads them, analysis shows that women are fully involved in every aspect of the work except the highest levels of administration. They teach in theological and Bible colleges, work alongside new and also long-established churches, and are involved in evangelism and lay-training, upgrading teaching and curricula for adult groups and Sunday Schools over wide areas. They translate the Bible, help to publish and sell Christian literature, and work in hospitals and schools, to name but a few callings. As they seek God's will for their work, it is not a matter of role or sex, but of gift and calling. They work alongside men as colleagues. As human beings, they do all that their male fellow workers do, and as women they do it according to their own special gifts. For decades we have prayed for more men, and for each man the Lord has called and sent two women, and through all three he has built his church overseas.

Are we so deaf that we cannot hear what he is trying to say to the churches in this country, bound by tradition, hierarchy and culture? Very few of those churches would ever think of using the spiritual gifts of these women as they are used overseas today, and the reason given is usually that it is not 'biblical'. Do we really believe there is one biblical principle for churches in this country and another for those overseas?

The way ahead

R. K. Johnston,[30] writing on 'The Role of Women in the Church and Family', challenges the inadequate hermeneutical principles used by evangelicals representing both the

[30] R. K. Johnston, *Evangelicals at an impasse*, p. 73.

egalitarian and traditional positions. (Too often a person's biblical 'interpretation' reflects primarily their denominational background.) He takes among others the key hermeneutical principle that 'insight into texts which are obscure must be gained from those which are plain'. He reminds us that in the current debate all three key passages – 1 Timothy 2; 1 Corinthians 11 and 14 –

> are extremely difficult to interpret: crucial words remain obscure (e.g. *authentein*; *exousia*); the addressed situations are difficult to reconstruct; the 'surface meaning' contradicts other Pauline material; and the methods of argument reflect cultural thought-forms no longer in use. Given these difficulties in interpreting the texts that seem most appropriate, the plain descriptions of Jesus' interaction with women and the stylised but readily interpreted accounts of woman's creation in Genesis take on an increased significance.

He pleads for specific texts to be expounded within the larger biblical themes of creation and redemption. If we begin our study where the Bible begins, and examine subsequent teaching and events in the light shed by creation principles, we may well find ourselves led to conclusions radically different from traditional interpretations. Paul Tournier has said:

> There are several ways of listening. You can listen in order to reply, or you can listen simply in order to hear. . . . Often we only half listen, more intent on thinking about our reply.[31]

We all need to learn to listen in order to understand what the other is saying. The present chapter has tried to explore some implications of creation too long neglected, and to examine the realities of life today for men and women.

If men can recognize that, when they operate without women, something is lacking, and if women can recognize that too often they shrug off God-given responsibilities

---

[31] P. Tournier, *The Gift of Feeling*, p. 103.

out of a mistaken view of femininity, then we can begin to discover how God calls us to serve him together in today's world.

Husband/wife relationships: a practical Christian viewpoint

Michael Griffiths

The problem expressed · Genesis and creation principles · Subjection · Authority · Headship · The practical outworking · Conclusion

Scripture is a challenge and a corrective to sloppy, culturally-determined traditions concerning the role of women. In relation to ministry, the commendation of the work of seven women in Romans 16 and two more in Philippians 4 as Paul's colleagues challenges traditional understanding of two brief and apparently negative passages. In relation to roles in marriage, Matthew 6:25, 31 challenges any view of the role of the woman which sees food, drink and clothes as her God-given concerns in life. Any view of the role of wives which restricts them to concerns which Christ described as pagan and banned for Christian disciples, female as well as male, must be suspect right from the start.

The problem expressed

This series on Christian differences allows me to express a strong viewpoint, knowing that it will be balanced by a different one.

I want to make this personal. I am intrigued to know whether my wife perceives herself differently from myself, because she lives inside a female body. None of us knows what it feels like to be someone else, but we know that each of us was 'fearfully and wonderfully made' (Ps.

139:14, AV) by our Creator, whether we are male or female. We do have a small chromosome difference, but we are both of the same species and I have no sound reason for believing that her consciousness is any different from mine, even if her hormones are different. The New Testament addresses us both alike as responsible children of God.

Just supposing, for a moment, that I was still myself, but living inside my wife's skin; would I, as a committed Christian, be content with household chores as my vocation? In view of Matthew 6:25, 31 would I appreciate being told that I should be content with cooking, cleaning, washing, ironing and mending for our family, with very restricted opportunities to go outside the home, create things, and be involved in interesting work useful to the church and wider society? Am I asking my wife to be content with a life-style which would bore me silly, if I were in her shoes? Certainly, I enjoy pottering around the house and garden doing odd chores. I find it quite relaxing. But suppose that I was expected to do that day in, day out, with little opportunity for any other outside ministry, and was told that I should accept this as my God-given role, because of my gender, how would I react? No amount of enthusing about the alleged glories of home-making and the wonder of being a woman would quite stifle my suspicion that this was all a big confidence trick to keep me content when I ought not to be content: because, as a disciple of Jesus, food, drink and clothes are, for me, pagan concerns. The Lord has called us, male and female alike, to seek first his kingdom and his righteousness.

How would I feel, inside my wife's skin, to be told that, however theologically trained and qualified I might be, it was improper for me to make verbal contributions in church? That however gifted I might be in speaking and preaching, it was not biblical for me to do either? And that the sole reason was my gender? The person that is me just could not be content, living in my wife's skin, to be patted patronizingly on the head for making tea and serving cakes, when I knew in my inward heart that I could serve the Lord fruitfully in other ways besides this. Suppose that I began to resent the straitjacket that some were making for me on allegedly (but mistakenly) biblical grounds; how would I feel to be told that I was rebelling against what Scripture said about my proper role as a wife?

It can be seen that this is not only a problem for a woman, but also for her caring husband, who ought to be concerned about the development and full deployment of his wife's spiritual gifts.

I was reading recently about the infuriated feelings of national Christians towards the maddening superior attitudes of some white missionaries, whose self-importance and clannishness made them feel excluded.[1] We all recognize that such a patronizing attitude towards fellow Christians is nauseating, wrong and racist. We also find a patronizing, superior attitude in some Christian men towards women, and is not that equally nauseating, wrong and sexist? Are not *both* only different forms of subcultural arrogance, and a manifestation of 'respect of persons' which is condemned by the standards of the Bible?

Let us look carefully then at various biblical strands of evidence.

Genesis and creation principles

> So God created man in his own image,
> in the image of God he created him;
> male and female he created them . . . (Gn. 1:27)

Mankind was created by God in two kinds, male and female, and there is no suggestion of priority of one sex over the other, but rather of parity and complementarity. The two together are created in the image of God, and both together are to 'rule' over the rest of creation (Gn. 1:26, 28).

Chapter 1 gives an account of creation as a whole and

[1] R. Pierce Beaver, *The Missionary between the Times* (Doubleday, 1968), p. 49.

the place of mankind in it. Chapter 2 focuses more closely upon mankind, and is thus like a second view of the same event taken with a close-up camera. Whereas everything that God had made was 'very good' (1:31), we are now told that the aloneness of the man is 'not good' (2:18). The first imperfection in God's creation is the absence of women. My wife in her article has dealt with these passages in much greater detail, but here it is sufficient to say that the expressions 'a *helper* suitable for him' (2:18) and 'suitable *helper*' (2:20) imply no inferiority in the woman. The same word is used fifteen times of God as the helper of his people, with no implications of inferiority!

The description of woman being made from man is manifestly pictorial (both sexes have the same number of ribs!) and the woman taken from the man is reunited with him, becoming 'one flesh' again in marriage (2:24). The intention of the passage appears to teach the close relationship of the sexes in marriage, and does not help us to know how men in general ought to relate to women in general. In Christian marriage, a man can say of only one woman that she is bone of his bone and flesh of his flesh. The only rule or dominion mentioned is that of male and female *together* over creation (1:28–29). To use any of these passages in trying to establish male superiority seems entirely gratuitous. The passages seem concerned rather to establish the close relationship between the two sexes, and the need of the man for the woman as his companion and complement.

It is sometimes argued that while the sexes were created equal, subjection was a result of the fall. It is not clear if 'your desire shall be for your husband, and he shall rule over you' (Gn. 3:16) is a prescriptive punishment or a descriptive statement. In any case it refers specifically to the sexual aspect of marriage, rather than to the total relationship. It is *not* how God created them 'in the beginning', and the new creation in Christ seems to have restored the original equality: 'neither . . . male nor female' (Gal. 3:28). Mrs Marlene Cohen, in her significant Australian NEAC address 'Marriage and Family in God's

Purposes',[2] writes: 'Neither bore a form of that image superior to the other's at creation, and neither retained a superior form of the image after the fall.'

The scarcity and brevity of the evidence, however, should be a warning to us all not to be dogmatic, nor to hang upon these verses conclusions that may be too heavy for them to bear. We *can* say that there is no necessary implication of the superiority or inferiority of either sex, and this is borne out by the clear statements of the New Testament (Gal. 3:28).

We turn then to the questions of 'subjection' and 'authority', two words often used in discussion of Christian roles within marriage, but as we shall see, often exaggerated and even misused.

Subjection

There is no doubt that the Bible does teach subjection in some sense, but what does that mean, and how is it relevant to marriage between Christians?

Firstly, *the Bible teaches subjection to the authority of the State* (Rom. 13:1; Tit. 3:1; 1 Pet. 2:13), which may or may not be a monarchy.

Secondly, *it teaches slaves to obey their earthly masters* with respect and fear (Eph. 6:5; Col. 3:22; 1 Tim. 6:1), and they are taught to be subject to their masters in everything, to try to please them, and not to talk back to them (Tit. 2:9; 1 Pet. 2:18).

Thirdly, *it teaches children to be subject to their parents*, Jesus himself being the supreme example of this (Lk. 2:51; 1 Tim. 3:4; Tit. 1:6).

Fourthly, and beyond dispute, *wives are told to be subject, but only to 'their own husbands'* (Eph. 5:22; Col. 3:18; Tit. 6:5; 1 Pet. 3:1, 5). It seems difficult to support the notion that the Bible teaches subjection of all women to all men. This notion is unpalatable to women (and unacceptable to most husbands!). The references all seem

[2] M. Cohen, 'Agenda for a Biblical Church' (*NEAC Report*, AIO, Sydney, 1981), Vol. 1, p. 143.

to stress that the wife is subject to her own chosen husband, rather than to other women's husbands.

Fifthly, *subjection is to operate within the churches and particularly to elders and church leaders* (1 Cor. 6:16; 1 Pet. 5:5; Heb. 13:17). Certain verses teach the submissiveness of women in a church context – not, unfortunately, our subject here (1 Cor. 14:34; 1 Tim. 2:11). But within the same church context is the injunction to all Christians generally to be 'subject to one another out of reverence for Christ' (Eph. 5:21). It is in this special context that the subsequent injunctions to wives to be subject to their husbands, children to obey their parents and slaves to obey their earthly masters, are given as particular illustrations of the way in which that general mutual submission is to operate among Christian believers.[3]

It seems worth stating the obvious, because it is possible to overlook it; namely, that the use of the same word for 'submission' does not appear to mean exactly the same thing in each of these five different categories. Nobody, one would hope, would want to identify the relationship of master and slave with the relationship of parent and child, and still less with that of husband and wife. Even though the same word may be used, even the most extreme 'male dominance is biblical' bigots surely cannot believe that a man's relationship with his wife is like that between a parent and child, or a master and a slave. While it is helpful to know that in derivation the word is used by the military about a 'subordinate' who is an 'inferior' in rank, this begs the whole question. Biblical first principles (Gn. 1:27, which teaches the parity of the sexes in creation, and Gal. 3:28, which teaches the parity of the sexes in salvation) do not allow us to regard the husband as being the superior to his wife, the inferior. As Hurley himself says,

Within the military model of authority, a general may

---

[3] J. B. Hurley is helpful here on the grammar, even if one does not accept his conclusions about the way in which the general command to mutual submission is modified by the subsequent injunctions. *Cf.* J. B. Hurley, *Man and Woman in Biblical Perspective* (IVP, 1981), pp. 140–141.

be authoritarian and a private bitter or passive without destroying their relation. This model simply will not work for sexual relations.[4]

Does Scripture contain any examples of mutual subordination between equals? It does, and this is therefore important in understanding 'subjection'. Let me suggest two examples. Firstly, the requirement that 'the spirits of the prophets [be] subject to the control of prophets' (1 Cor. 14:32) appears to demand a mutual subordination between equals. You cannot refer to the prophet who is submitting to another prophet as being the 'subordinate' any more than the wife can properly be regarded as her husband's 'subordinate'. Secondly,

> . . . Each man should have his own wife, and each woman her own husband. The husband should fulfil his marital duty to his wife, and likewise the wife to her husband. The wife's body does not belong to her alone but also to her husband. In the same way, the husband's body does not belong to him alone but also to his wife (1 Cor. 7:2–4, NIV).

The sexual relationship between husband and wife is seen as one of mutual subjection. The husband and wife have an equal authority over each other's bodies.

The Ephesian context (Eph. 5:21ff.) puts the subjection of wives to husbands into a dependent clause of the main statement that we as Christians are all to be subject one to another. This suggests that we must (*pace* Hurley) also read the total husband/wife relationship in the context of a mutual subjection to each other, even though this is less apposite to the parent/child and master/slave relationship. While it may be true that God's relation to his people is likened to that of a husband to his wife, nowhere in Scripture is the husband himself likened to God!

It is very important to notice that there are always biblical limits to each of these categories of subjection.

Firstly, in relation to the State, *Peter and John specifically repudiated subjection when to obey the secular*

[4] J. B. Hurley, *op. cit.*, p. 149.

authorities meant to disobey God (Acts 4:19).

Secondly, *the master/slave relationship also had its limits* (in Israel, at any rate): slaves could not be expected to work more than six days a week (Ex. 20:10): and only until the next year of release, a maximum of six years (Ex. 21:2; Dt. 15:12–18), when they were to be given sufficient assets to make a fresh start. They were to be given their freedom if a brutal master knocked out a tooth (Ex. 21:26–27), and not returned to their masters if they ran away (Dt. 23:15), while kidnappers who sold others into slavery merited the death sentence (Ex. 21:16; Dt. 24:7). Thus, in the Jewish biblical tradition the submission claimed by masters over slaves was far from absolute. The fact that slavery has now been officially abolished in the world raises questions as to whether it is legitimate to argue at all about husband/wife relationships on a basis of an abolished relationship – even while agreeing with Hurley that parent/child and husband/wife relationships cannot be abolished.

Thirdly, *there are also limits to a parents' claim on the obedience of their children*, evident in the teaching of Jesus, that he had come to set a man against his father and mother, and that those not prepared to 'hate' their fathers and mothers (that is, if they oppose their conversion) were not fit to be disciples at all. Evidently, in all these other relationships there are limits to the authority of the State, the authority of masters, and the authority of parents; and their authority has to be refused in matters of principle. The same is even true in our fifth category of authority in the church, where, interestingly, Paul refused to give 'subjection' (Gal. 2:5) to the apostolic church leaders in Jerusalem when they were wrong in principle.

It is surely, then, legitimate to argue that there must be some limits to the extent to which wives are to be subject to their own husbands. Scripture does say 'submit to [your] husbands in everything' (Eph. 5:24), but does that mean that there are no limits?

In fact, Scripture itself shows that there are limits: Sapphira was held responsible for accepting her husband, Ananias', deception: she should not have been subject to him in that (Acts 4:1, 2, 9). Abraham, whom Sarah his wife obeyed and called 'Lord', was on one occasion explicitly told to do 'whatever Sarah tells you' (Gn. 21:12). And that was to apply, even when what she wanted, namely the sending away of Hagar and her boy (also Abraham's son) into the desert without water and protection, seems thoroughly cruel and irresponsible (and, according to the Nuzi texts, probably illegal). Abigail was certainly not being subject to her churlish husband, Nabal, when she helped David and his men after Nabal had refused to do so (1 Sa. 25:17). But she is commended for her wisdom.

In summary, then, we should not exalt the concept of 'subjection' of a wife as an absolute, but recognize that it must be modified by the biblical considerations elaborated above. It would appear to be a voluntary subjection which a woman makes to her own husband, and not to men in general. Further, in the same passage about the subjection of the wife (Eph. 5), the husband is commanded to love his wife as Christ loved the church and gave himself for it. This again sets limits to the degree to which a husband can expect his wife to submit to him, if he fails to love her and to give himself sacrificially for her.

> As Christ first gave himself, so husbands are to first give themselves. The church is to respond to Christ in self giving: wives are to give themselves in response to their husbands. There is no chicken-and-egg debate here. The order is clear. Husbands who want to be in line with the general teaching and the specific example of Christ must make the first move.[5]

Authority

The word 'authority' is frequently bandied about in discussions on husband/wife relationships. About this, several things could be said: firstly, that between Christians 'authority' is not a way of 'lording over' people in the way that Gentile cultures do, but the way of humble service

[5] M. Cohen, 'Agenda for a Biblical Church' (*NEAC Report*), Vol. 1, p. 152.

(Lk. 22:24–27). The Gentile form of authority is forbidden to disciples in general, regardless of their sex.

Secondly, reference to a concordance suggests that this concept does not bear the weight which some people would like to hang upon it. It is hardly ever used at all in the context of husband/wife relations. The word *exousia* usually translated as 'authority' or 'right' is a common word in the New Testament, occurring more than 100 times, but in only two places with any direct reference to wives or women. One is the extremely enigmatic verse about women covering their heads as a symbol of authority (1 Cor. 11:10), where all the commentators get into real difficulties, and where it possibly means her own authority. The second verse is most relevant: 'a wife has no authority over her own body, but the husband, and in the same way the husband has no authority over his own body, but his wife' (1 Cor. 7:4). Here the authority is manifestly reciprocal and cannot be used to suggest the husband has some authority over his wife which his wife does not have equally over him. It really is here a mutual submission that is called for in the sexual relationship. It comes as something of a shock, when one remembers how frequently the subject of 'authority' is referred to in the context of marriage, to discover that the notion has so little support from the Bible itself.

In some translations 1 Timothy 2:12 translates the word *authentein* as 'usurp authority', and Paul says that he does not permit a wife (or woman) to teach or *domineer over* her husband (or man). The word is a very nasty one, meaning to dominate and contradict. Since domineering is forbidden to all Christians in their relationships to one another, we are all bound to agree entirely with the apostle, but we should surely not reverse this understanding to mean that he wants *men* to domineer over their *wives*!

Archbishop Donald Robinson, replying to Mrs Cohen, says:

> I agree with Mrs Cohen that 'any exercise of personal rule over each other in relationships is anathema to

Michael Griffiths

the whole thrust of the New Testament', so long as by 'personal rule' we mean acting in self-interest or in a usurped position of superiority.[6]

Headship

The idea of man being 'the head' also needs to be considered carefully. It is used both in 1 Corinthians 11:3 and Ephesians 5:23, where in both places we can translate 'head of the wife'. We are also told that the head of Christ is God (1 Cor. 11:3), where we know that the Persons of the Trinity are equal and that 'head' in this sense cannot mean that one party is 'greater' than the other. The difficulty here is to disengage that section of our thinking which attributes twentieth-century English language connotations to 'head' when trying to understand what the Bible says.

The Greeks apparently did not use the word 'head' in the sense of 'headmaster' or headman, while the significance of the 'head' of a body was not appreciated anatomically in New Testament times (according to Moule[7]) as suggesting control or direction of the body by the mind. They did use the word for 'origin', so that the word could be used for the source of a river, much as we talk of the 'head waters'. There is no necessary implication of inferiority, then, in suggesting that the head of Christ is God, and the head of a wife is her husband. Hurley is probably right in suggesting that 'origin' is less satisfactory as a translation in Ephesians 5 than in 1 Corinthians 11, where Paul balances the idea of reminding his readers not only that man is the origin of woman in the Genesis 2 account of creation, but that in fact every subsequent man has found his origin in a woman (1 Cor. 11:12).

Mary Evans is most helpful on headship.[8] She points

[6] D. W. B. Robinson, 'Agenda for a Biblical Church' (*NEAC Report*), Vol. 2, p. 161.

[7] C. F. D. Moule, *The Epistles of Paul the Apostle to the Colossians and Philemon* (CUP, 1957), p. 68.

[8] M. Evans, *Women: in Biblical Perspective* (London University M. Phil. thesis, 1977), pp. 67ff.

out that a first-century metaphor in Greek need not be identified with twentieth-century usage in English. The metaphor, in any case, is original to Paul and not found in other contemporary literature. Chrysostom thought that the concept of head spoke primarily of the *union* of the head with the body.

In Ephesians the headship of the husband is found together with the concept of the subjection of the wife. However, the analogy of the headship of Christ over the church is not interpreted in terms of authority (although he has this, as its Saviour), but rather in terms of his loving and giving himself on behalf of the church. This implies, therefore, that the husband's headship must be understood to mean 'loving and giving'.

Ephesians 5:24 begins in Greek with the strong adversative 'but' (*alla*), although this is omitted in many Bible translations (the AV seems quite wrong in changing it to 'therefore'). This means that we should read the text as, 'The husband is head of the wife . . . *but* as the church is subject to Christ, so let wives be subject.' In other words, because headship implies loving and giving rather than authority, the husband is to love and serve his wife certainly, *but* even though he is a loving and giving head, she is also to be subject to him. It seems, then, that 'headship' does not necessarily imply authority, otherwise this 'but' would be unnecessary. Mary Evans sums this up by saying:

> It is often suggested that the use of such terms as 'head' and 'submission' is evidence that Paul did see a hierarchical order in marriage, but we have shown that these terms are not necessarily used in that way. Rather, Paul emphasized the total responsibility of each partner towards their spouse.[9]

Finally, we should notice that Scripture never suggests that a husband is to 'subject' his wife to himself: in the Bible only God subjects others to himself in this way (1 Cor. 15:27–28; Eph. 1:22; Phil. 3:21). This is a neces-

---

[9] *Ibid.*, p. 88.

sary caution, because a certain type of insecure husband may batten on to unbalanced 'authority' teaching and be so ill-advised as to say to his partner, 'You are supposed to submit to me': an approach quite inconsistent with a genuinely reciprocal marriage relationship. One well-known teacher in North America on the proper line of authority (God-man-woman-child-dawg!) goes so far as to teach that a wife should never disagree with her husband's opinions (he happens to have remained a bachelor!)

> Headship does not sanctify masculine desires to dominate as though it is the male prerogative to exercise power over others, as though the male is to subdue and the female is to be subdued.[10]

The practical outworking

I am glad that my wife teaches me many things! What impoverished kind of marriage relationship is it indeed, where a man does not learn a great deal from his wife? A wife's wisdom helps to moderate her husband when he is over-reacting. Who else is there, close enough to observe the husband's failures, and intimate enough to reprove and rebuke them without spoiling the relationship? Christian marriage is a mutual relationship, where God uses each partner to bless the other. The more extreme teaching about 'authority' impoverishes the marriage relationship by making it less reciprocal.

The only experience of marriage that anybody has is their own. Speaking personally, we found that working together as married fellow workers in isolated missionary areas deepened our mutual respect. We belonged to a Missionary Society which screened both of us, and designated both of us. It also stressed unanimity in decision-making, and did not normally move forward without agreement. We also, within our marriage, have found it sensible to move forward only when the two of us are agreed. It might sometimes have been easier for me as the

[10] J. W. Wilson, 'Agenda for a Biblical Church' (*NEAC Report*), Vol. 2, p. 153.

husband to have made unilateral decisions. But to have introduced the concept of unilateral subjection (not, as we have seen, a scriptural concept at all) would have meant that our decisions were no longer joint decisions between equal partners. The apostle Paul spoke of women as being his colleagues (fellow workers) in Romans 16:3 and Philippians 4:3, where he also calls them members of the same team (*synethlesan*). The missionary wife is a fellow worker, and the apostle Peter seems to have shared such partnership as he led his wife around on his travels (1 Cor. 9:5) and he speaks of husbands and wives being 'joint-heirs of the grace of life' (1 Pet. 3:7).

It is commonly maintained that the purpose of 'subjection' is that, when a disagreement occurs between husbands and wives which cannot be resolved, then the machinery should already exist for the man to give the casting vote. On paper this sounds fine, but how often in practice does this have to happen? There is no evidence from the Bible and certainly none from objective psychological criteria to suggest that the man has a monopoly of intelligence and wisdom. Certainly the Bible (Pr. 31) suggests that a woman has a great deal to contribute to marriage.

If a woman is extremely unhappy about a course of action that her husband wishes to follow or the decision he wishes to make, then surely love and consideration for her, and the Christian responsibility to be mutually subjected to one another, will make him reconsider. He will surely endeavour to find a compromise, or a way of meeting his life partner's misgivings. To be 'joint-heirs of the grace of life' (1 Pet. 3:7) implies a partnership in which both contribute differently but equally.

The woman may be a weaker vessel now, although it is not quite clear in what sense that is meant, for while in western cultures there may be more burly men than burly women, in other cultures there are many burly women navvies and farm labourers. She is not weaker in brains or gifts, or in courage and endurance. She would be weaker while carrying children, but the force here may be that she would be weaker legally in first-century Asia

Minor, whereas in heaven she would inherit equally with her husband.

There are obviously widely different cultural ways in which the sexes relate to each other in different ethnic situations and even within different sub-cultures in the same society. When it comes to settling disagreements, however, one notices that even when people sincerely believe that one partner is meant to be dominant, biblically, in practice they settle for a *modus vivendi*.

As a husband I feel astonished gratitude that any woman would be willing to lay aside, for the years of child-bearing and rearing at least, all her other prospects: the possibility of earning a salary, equal to any man's, of living an independent life, of using the gifts that God has given her; and to lay all that aside in order to share life with me, to help me, and to work with me.

There is a division of labour in any marriage, and couples may come to differing conclusions about the way in which they will divide the work of the home. Most couples will agree that the husband should equally serve his wife by hard physical work in house and garden. It is humbling that another independent human being, created by God to rule over creation, should wash, iron and mend my clothes along with her own, not just once to show her love, but unremittingly, year after year. And while I do express appreciation sometimes, it would be fatally easy to adopt the unthinking attitude that it is her role and responsibility to do that for me.

But isn't it a most remarkable and humbling thing, that another human being should give her time and energy, just as precious as my own, to do these practical things for the two of us? Teaching which says that this is properly what she is supposed to be doing, because this is her God-ordained role, diminishes that sense of love and gratitude which I ought to feel.

The more extreme teaching helps us not at all with the problems of the captive housewife, tied up all day in the home with small children, fearful of becoming an intellectual cabbage. Of course, young children need the attention of mother at home, but in these days with the emphasis on zero-population growth and smaller families, a woman may have all her children out at school all day, well before she is forty years of age. How is she now to develop as a person? Her intelligence is equal to her husband's, and her capacity for creativity at least as great. (I know of no statistics which prove that the female population is significantly less intelligent than the male, and pre-war intelligence tests suggested the opposite!) Her work capacity and her energies are at least equal to mine. For all that Scripture says about the woman being the 'weaker vessel', many modern housewives, even with labour-saving devices, expend more muscular energy in the home than do husbands in sedentary office jobs.

Are we really to make out that *Scripture* says that she is to stay quietly at home, being allegedly 'feminine', cooking meals and mending clothes for her lord and master who is busy about his own affairs and leaves her there to stew in her loneliness? To suggest that a woman's role is properly to give herself solely to the domestic matters of preparing meals and thinking about clothes, is not only to cramp a gifted woman cruelly, but to distort and to deny what Jesus commanded for all disciples, both male and female, when he instructed them to 'take no thought for what you shall eat and drink and put on'. If it is wrong for a Christian man to be obsessed with food and clothes, it is equally wrong for a Christian woman.

Nobody is disputing that a woman's life is affected by the responsibilities of being a wife and mother, but she should nonetheless develop all her gifts and potential to the full. It is the responsibility of her husband-man to see that this happens. I was once saying at a meeting that 'a husband should be just as concerned about the development of his wife's natural and spiritual gifts as he is about his own'. Then I realized that my wife was sitting at the back of the meeting and I was giving her little opportunity to develop her own gifts. It was one of those occasions when you hear the Lord's quiet words in your heart, 'Thou art the man', and feel convicted, as David did by Nathan's words.

While some women exercise a wide ministry centred on

111

their homes, that does not mean that other women with different gifts should be held back from going out and doing other things. They may prove much better and more stimulating life partners when they are encouraged to develop wider interests beyond the limits of the house in which they live. The idea of 'home' should not be equated, surely, with the bricks and mortar of a house.

Conclusion

The teaching of Scripture on marriage is wonderfully healthy and wholesome. There is, sadly, a danger that some will take a shallow understanding of a few proof texts to espouse a narrow, authoritarian, male-dominated view of marriage which cannot be sustained when the whole of Scripture is looked at carefully. Women are disciples, saints, kings and priests, no less than their husbands. It is sub-Christian to 'subject' women, to dominate them and to treat them as being a lesser sub-species of human being, because women too are made in the image of God.

Response to
Michael Griffiths

David Field

Some authors are impressive from a distance, but disappointing when you get closer and discover that their life-style does not measure up to their eloquence. Michael Griffiths is not like that! He writes about family relationships from within the experience of a beautiful marriage. Anyone who has spent time in the Griffiths' home listens with enormous respect to what Michael and Valerie have to say about married life.

At the risk of being expelled from the series, I must record four points where I find myself agreeing almost totally with Michael's presentation.

1. The two of us agree that *roles in marriage should not be tied to gender*. The 'captive wife' stereotype is a caricature of biblical teaching. Of course, God means every married woman to use her gifts and develop her potential to the full! I would go a step further, and say that it is one of her husband's major responsibilities as 'head' to make sure that she has freedom to do exactly that.

2. We agree that *all ideas of superiority and inferiority in marriage are unscriptural*. Whatever the Bible means by the husband 'being head' and the wife 'being subject', it does not imply that he is superior to her in status. That is blatant sexism, and Scripture condemns it.

3. We agree that *cultural conditioning deeply affects our attitudes and outlook*. Here Michael, with his global experience, speaks with far more authority than I can muster. As an insular English stay-at-home, I react with amazement to press photographs of Russian women digging up roads and piloting helicopters. But I have to accept that their cultural understanding of gender roles is as valid as mine.

4. I agree with Michael that *marriage is for mutual education*. A Christian husband is misunderstanding headship completely if he resents his wife's criticisms and thinks he has nothing to learn from her. There is all the difference in the world between a Christian home and a chauvinist sty.

Nevertheless (relax, Editor!), there are three doubts I have to record. The first two are no more than niggles. The third is a major point of difference.

1. It worries me when we decry traditionally 'feminine' roles to boost the more 'masculine' ones we want women to share. Why reduce home-making to doing household chores? Why contrast housekeeping with 'interesting' work, 'useful' to the church and wider society? That kind of teaching pulls the mat from underneath the Bible's teaching on vocation. If God is calling me, either as husband or wife, to cook, clean, polish, scrub, wash, iron and mend things, then that is a role that is every bit as valuable – in his sight – as dictating a creative article or playing with a computer. Whether I *enjoy* doing the things I do is irrelevant. Their value lies in my being called to do them by God.

2. The argument from cultural conditioning can be taken in more than one way. We have certainly inherited a hierarchical view of family life, and if we are middle-aged we are very likely to see this as normal (and therefore right!). I am middle-aged, so I may be misguided. Nevertheless, the culture that I (and most readers of this book) know best does not favour hierarchies any longer. The fashionable thing to do today is to challenge authority structures, not accept them. Culturally speaking, anyone

who champions the idea of headship in marriage is on a hiding to nothing. And that applies, in my experience, inside church circles as well as outside them. It is at least open to question, whether marriages are stronger or weaker as a result. I am sure Michael would agree with me that as Christians we are called to judge any cultural expressions of married life by biblical standards, not vice versa. Are we, in the West, selling out to the anti-authoritarian spirit of our age?

3. Thirdly – and this is the big one – I believe that the Bible teaches that the authority of headship *complements* the loving unity every married couple is meant to enjoy.

Here is the vital difference between Michael Griffiths' position and my own. He sees an 'either-or' in Scripture where I find a 'both-and'. He writes, 'Headship implies loving and giving, *rather than* authority' (italics mine); whereas I hold that all three ideas – loving, giving and authority – belong together under the Bible's 'headship' umbrella. He treats submission and inferiority as the same thing; whereas I want to distinguish sharply between them.

I have read Michael's supporting arguments, including the suggestions that 'submit' and 'head' do not mean quite what they seem to mean. I confess that I remain unconvinced. To my mind, he has set up an Aunt Sally (or rather, a chauvinist Uncle Worzel), and demolished it with an enthusiasm that I totally share. My own case for what I conceive to be genuine, rather than abused, headship has already been set out. You, the reader, must judge between us.

Response to
Valerie Griffiths

Elizabeth Catherwood

It is impossible in a few words to comment on all the points where I think differently from Valerie Griffiths, so I shall mention only a few which have struck me most forcibly.

1. Valerie seems to be suggesting that *the cross has brought about a change in the* order *of marriage*. While I would totally agree that the love of God 'shed abroad in our hearts' has changed our *attitudes* in marriage, is not the whole biblical picture that the purpose of God from the beginning was the headship of the man? *Cf.* John Stott again: 'Creationism not chauvinism'. Further, as with fallen nature, sickness, death, and the 'sweat of the brow' in general, even the results of the fall still remain with women.

2. The paragraphs on *ishsha*, and 'a helper fit for him', *etc.*, would seem to illustrate again *the danger of basing an argument, even partly, on single words*. As with economists, when you get two Hebrew experts you get three opinions. Gordon Wenham,[1] Werner Neuer,[2] S. B. Clark[3]

[1] G. Wenham, 'The Ordination of Women', *Churchman* 92, 4, 1978.
[2] W. Neuer, *Mann und Frau in Biblischer Sicht* (1982).
[3] S. B. Clark, *Man and Woman in Christ* (Servant Books, 1980).

and J. T. Walsh,[4] equally basing their opinions on the words used, demonstrate that from the beginning God ordained the headship of the man. In our interpretation of Scripture, we need to grasp the big general principles in its teaching. While agreeing about the difficulty over *authentein* and *exousia*, I do wonder sometimes whether perhaps those passages are not more difficult to *accept* than to interpret, especially when 1 Timothy 5, Titus 2, and the passages in Ephesians and Colossians are all basically saying the same thing.

3. *Can we as evangelicals really avoid any biblical teaching by saying that it reflects outmoded 'cultural thought forms'*, or accept that the great Genesis history is 'stylized'? Strangely enough, my feeling is that such arguments fail above all to expound the texts (as R. K. Johnston himself pleads) within the 'larger biblical themes of creation and redemption'.

4. I am sorry that the only reference to Calvin by Valerie Griffiths (and by David Field) should be the translated quotation, *'appendage to the man'*. My translation of his commentary on Genesis 2 says that woman is an *accession* to the man. It is in a passage where Calvin is underlining that woman, too, is created in the image of God – 'whence it follows that what was said of the creation of the man belongs to the female sex.' He has earlier attacked those who have 'defined that to be a happy life, which is passed without a wife'. To those 'wicked suggestions of Satan', Calvin replies that God 'ordains the conjugal life for man, not to his destruction, but to his salvation'. Calvin is a much maligned man.

5. Michael Griffiths makes an admirable appeal to husbands to exercise kindness, but I feel that *occasionally his case is overstated by his use of non-biblical pejorative words, e.g.* 'dominant'. Also, don't most 'fellow workers' have a leader? Furthermore (regarding the limits of a wife's submission, if her husband is not Christ-like in his love), Peter urges Christian wives to submit to husbands who

---

[4] J. T. Walsh, 'Genesis 2:4 – 3:24', *Journal of Biblical Literature* 76, 1977.

'do not believe the word'.

6. Perhaps the overall difference between us is that *we are addressing different audiences*. The Griffithses are speaking to men who are abusing their God-given role and keeping women down unbiblically and unjustly. I, on the other hand, have in mind strident, assertive, 'I must be free to develop myself' women, whom I am meeting in increasing numbers, in every kind of Christian circle.

Part 2

Women in ministry

Women in the church

Women's ministry:
a new look at the biblical texts

The role of women in the church

Women in ministry

James B. Hurley

*The task · Women in patriarchal times · Women and
ministry in the Mosaic period · In the time of Christ ·
In Jesus' life and teaching · In the life of the apostolic
church · In the teaching of the apostolic church ·
Elders and deacons in 1 Timothy 3 · In conclusion*

The task

In an effort to discover what the Bible has to say with
regard to the role of women in ministry, I will seek in this
essay to study the roles of men and women in biblical
revelation and to distil principles which will help us to
relate such findings to the present.[1]

Women in patriarchal times

Although we have relatively little data about the patriarchal period between the fall and the exodus, we can draw
a certain number of conclusions. Noah, Abraham, Isaac,
Jacob and his sons all functioned as patriarchs, leading
their households. In their lives there was an overlapping
of the civil, family and religious aspects of life. Family
units constituted the civic and religious communities as
well. This fact makes it difficult to separate, for instance,
Abraham's roles as priest, patriarch, prophet, father and
husband. When he received a message from God about
where to move, was he a leader of his small nation (tribe),

---

[1] Subjects and texts treated in this essay receive more thorough treatment in my book *Man and Woman in Biblical Perspective. A study in
role relations and authority* (IVP (UK)/Zondervan (USA), 1981).

a husband, or a prophet? Probably he was all three.

On a private level, we see the women of the patriarchal period dealing directly with God. When the Lord visits Abraham at the Oaks of Mamre, Sarah laughs at God's promise and communicates directly with him (denying her laughter) (Gn. 18:15). Hagar sees and talks with God during her flight from Sarah (Gn. 16:7–14). Rachel rejoices that God has heard her when her handmaid bears a son (Gn. 30:6).

There was no temple ministry in this period and public worship was led by the senior male of a tribal unit, who functioned as its priest. Thus Noah led his family in sacrifice as they left the ark, and God made his covenant with Abraham, Isaac and Jacob, who in turn built altars at which to worship the Lord. In these activities the patriarchs did not represent themselves only, but their families as well; the promises of God are clearly both for them and for their seed after them.

We do not see women priests or matriarchs in the patriarchal period. It has sometimes been concluded from this that 'men' were priests and 'women' were not. I believe that this way of stating it is a mistake. The senior male of a household was priest for *all* of its members, male and female alike. This is not sexist in the usual twentieth-century use of the term. *Certain* men acted as priests for other men *and* women.

The patriarchal priests had a particular ministry in the worship of God. What did the rest of the people do? Scripture does not provide us with elaborate answers, but it is clear that all believers were called, as was Abraham, to keep the covenant, to walk before God and to be perfect (Gn. 17:1). This ministry of life came equally to the men and to the women.

Women and ministry in the Mosaic period

God's organization of Israel after the exodus gives us a clearer set of distinctions between family, state and religious aspects of culture. It is thus easier to ask what the ministry of women was in this period.

Women in ministry

The entire nation of Israel was called to love and to obey the Lord and to be a demonstration of his grace. Both men and women possessed civil roles and could partake in commerce, inheritance and government (Pr. 31; Nu. 27:1–11; 30:3–17; Jdg. 4; 5; 2 Ki. 11:3). In addition God raised up women prophets (2 Ki. 22:14, 19–20; Jdg. 4:4–6).

In the religious sphere, all Israelites were called upon to enter into a personal relationship with God. All might come to the tabernacle and later to the temple to worship, to fulfil vows and to offer sacrifices. In these areas of service, all were equal.

It is as we consider the public exercise of religion (cultic activities) that we begin to perceive differences between Israelites. All Israelites worshipped God; men and women sang in the choirs; and a group of women 'ministered at the door of the tent of meeting' (Ex. 38:8; cf. also 1 Ch. 25:5–6; 2 Ch. 35:25). But the Lord claimed every firstborn male for his own service. In the Mosaic legislation, all the unblemished (not physically deformed) males of the tribe of Levi were taken in the stead of the firstborn males (Nu. 3:12–13).

Of the Levites set apart to God's service, only those of the house of Aaron could be priests (Ex. 28:1–3). Even this restricted number was not free to serve at will. Specific regulations were set down concerning the sequence of their serving and the conditions of ceremonial cleanliness required of those who served (Lv. 21ff.).

These Mosaic restrictions set apart *certain* men to serve as representatives and leaders in the worship of Israel. Once again, the laws are not sexist in modern terms. The principle was not that men could, but women could not, serve. It was rather that God called out certain men to serve in particular functions. All deformed Aaronic men, all other men and all women were not called to be priests.

The selection of Moses, Aaron and Aaron's sons for special roles did not go unnoticed. Korah and a large number of well-known Israelites challenged the exclusive 'right' of Moses, Aaron and the house of Aaron to serve as leaders. Their complaint was couched in democratic terms: 'The whole community is holy, every one of them, and the Lord is with them. Why then do you set yourselves above the Lord's assembly?' (Nu. 16:3). In response to this contemporary-sounding complaint, Moses replied: 'Listen, you Levites! Isn't it enough for you that God has separated you from the rest of the Israelite community . . . It is against the Lord that you . . . have banded together. Who is Aaron that you should gamble against him?' (Nu. 16:8–9, 11, NIV).

Korah and his followers looked at the priesthood as a mark of dignity and personal worth. They felt demeaned, having been excluded. But was God saying that Aaron was chosen because he was better qualified? Think for a minute about Aaron's 'qualifications'. He had made a golden calf idol (Ex. 32). His sons sinfully brought strange fire before the Lord (Lv. 10:1). Notwithstanding these sins, it was God's pleasure to call Aaron and his sons to serve. Their call was not a statement about their better qualification or personal superiority.

Women of the Mosaic period participated freely in many areas of Israelite life. In private worship and most aspects of public religious life, they were on equal footing with men. Only in the levitical service in the tabernacle/temple and in the priesthood was there a differentiation. Certain men were called out to serve as leaders and representatives of the people in the cultic affairs. All women and all other men were holy, members of God's people, but not called to be priests or Levites. With regard to representative, male leadership in public religious functions, the Mosaic administration of God's covenant is perfectly in line with the patriarchal administration.

Women and ministry in the time of Christ

Between the close of the Old Testament and beginning of the New Testament, significant events happened within the Jewish nation. The exile, Roman rule and foreign cultural influences led to a retrenchment in social customs and to a different view of women. Women were increasingly seen as less intelligent than men and as sources of sexual temptation. Josephus, a Jewish historian and a contemporary of Paul, wrote, 'the woman is inferior to the man in every way.'[2]

This strong view is echoed in the writings of the *Talmud*, a collection of Jewish wisdom dating from before Christ to the sixth century, which classifies women with slaves and heathen and assumes them incapable of learning.[3] Rabbi Jose ben Johana (*c.* 150 BC) is quoted as saying 'He that talks much with women brings evil on himself . . . and at last will inherit Gehenna'.[4]

With such an attitude towards women, it is not surprising to find that women played little role in the social life of the time, or in the worship and ministry of Judaism. Although they could attend worship, it was not required of them except on certain occasions.[5] Women could not lead in worship and even the oral reading of the Scripture was not for them. Eliezer ben Azariah's comment about women attending the reading of the Law in obedience to the command of Deuteronomy 31:10–13 reflects the attitude of many rabbis: 'the men came to learn, the women came to hear'.[6]

It is against such a background that the ministry of Jesus is to be considered.

Women and ministry in Jesus' life and teaching

Jesus was not a man bound by tradition. In his life and ministry we find him consistently framing his actions by his own theology rather than by that of his contemporaries. This is overwhelmingly true in his approach to women. The most surprising aspect of his dealing with women is the fact of their natural presence in all that he did. The crowds which followed him included women, whom Jesus taught and considered to be his disciples alongside the men (Mt. 12:49–50). In Luke 8 we read of

[2] *Contra Apiones*, 2, 201.
[3] bMen. 43a, b; bHag. 3a; 4a; bYom. 66b.
[4] mAb. 1.5; *cf.* also bKidd. 70a, b; 81a; bErub. 53b; bEer. 43b; mKidd. 4.12.
[5] bHag. 3a.   [6] bHag. 3a.

a group of women who travelled with Jesus (probably raising some observers' eyebrows!) and supported him from their means.

Luke 10:38–42 provides us with a special piece of information about Jesus' friends. In this familiar passage Martha frets about the fact that her sister Mary is sitting at Jesus' feet learning, while she does the dirty work alone. Jesus rebukes Martha for choosing to pursue the housework instead of learning, and commends Mary for having made a better choice. He is not commending Mary's avoidance of work, but affirming the importance of learning from the Saviour while he is on earth. Note that Luke did not find it unusual that Mary would be seated at Jesus' feet learning, nor that Jesus considered Mary's wise choice one that Martha too should have made. Whereas synagogue instruction was exclusively by and for men, and some rabbis announced that 'it is better that the words of the Law should be burned than that they should be given to a woman',[7] Jesus regularly taught women the truth of God.

The place occupied by women in Jesus' ministry stands in marked contrast to their place in the Jewish society of his day and in the *Talmud* (although not in such marked contrast to their role in the Old Testament). From his teaching and practice we can see that Jesus treated men and women as persons needing God's grace. Jesus did not structurally organize his church during his earthly ministry. It is to the post-resurrection church that we must turn to learn how the Lord is pleased to order his church.

Women and ministry in the life of the apostolic church

The unprecedented role of women in the ministry of Christ continued into the life of the Christian church without debate or remark. The women who accompanied the Lord in his travels and observed his death for sinners continued with the disciples after the resurrection (Acts 1:13–14). When the Holy Spirit came, the tongues of fire settled, as Joel had prophesied, upon both the men and women (Acts

---

[7] Josephus, *Antiquities*, 16.164; mSot. 4.3; mKidd. 4.13; jSot. 3.4.

2:1–4, 17–18). Luke carefully informs us that the Lord added both men and women to his church both in Jerusalem and in Samaria (Acts 5:14; 8:12). The women so added had a privilege which Jewish women did not enjoy in the synagogues; all of the believers were taught (Acts 2:42).

It was not only among the churches of the disciples that women enjoyed a new role. Paul, that old chauvinist rabbi, was notably Christian rather than rabbinic in his attitude to women. Everywhere he went they were included in the churches: Philippi, Thessalonica, Berea, Athens, Corinth (Acts 16:13–16; 17:4, 12, 34; 18:2). Paul not only included women, he sought them out and taught them. It required ten adult, free men to start a Jewish synagogue (mMeg. 4.3). Children, slaves and women did not count. When Paul went to the place of prayer by the river at Philippi he met with the *women* who gathered there. There were too few men in Philippi to start a synagogue. The nucleus of Paul's church was drawn from this group of women. One, Lydia, became the hostess of the church.

The women of the apostolic churches were more than hearers or even learners of the Word. They were doers also. What they did is a matter of record, aspects of which we must now examine.

Love in-deed

The early Christians were noted for their charity. The needs of the widows, orphans, poor and imprisoned were by no means unnoticed. Both men and women played a part. The 'deacons' of Acts 6 supervised the feeding of thousands of believers. The widows of 1 Timothy 5:9 lived exemplary lives of concern for others. Tabitha (Dorcas) provided services for the poor in Joppa (Acts 9:36–43). These persons were engaged in ministry in the biblical sense of the word. *Diakonia*, the Greek word translated 'ministry', means service. The prime example of such serving ministry in the New Testament is the Lord himself who 'did not come to be ministered unto [served], but to minister [serve] and even to give his life as a ransom for many' (Mt. 20:28).

Worship

Worship is also a form of 'service'. Whereas Jewish women did not need to attend worship and could not participate vocally in it, the Christian women participated freely in worship, prayer and prophecy (1 Cor. 11:5; Acts 21:9) and joined others in bringing a hymn, a word of instruction, a revelation, a tongue or an interpretation (1 Cor. 14:26). As the various members of the congregation did this, others were to receive their words or songs respectfully, submitting themselves to one another out of reverence for Christ (Eph. 5:19–21).

Missionary service; fellow workers

In the vocabulary of Paul there are few titles more significant than that of 'fellow worker'. He wrote 'Greet Prisca [diminutive: Priscilla] and Aquila, my fellow workers in Christ Jesus. They risked their lives for me. Not only I but all the churches of the Gentiles are grateful to them' (Rom. 16:3–5, NIV). The same term is used of men such as Timothy and Titus as well as of women such as Euodia and Syntyche. These are persons who have shared with Paul in the hard and dangerous work of announcing God's saving message. We are not told by Paul what roles these women and men had. It is likely that their specific roles were as varied as their gifts, and that both the men and the women shared the gospel with any who would listen.

In Romans 16 Paul sends greetings to twenty-six persons at Rome. Of the twenty-six, eight are women. Of the eight, six receive individual attention. Women played a prominent role in Paul's ministry.

Church officers

In recent years the question of the role of women in the formal offices of the church has received much attention. Throughout the history of the church, an overwhelming majority of Christians have believed that only some of the men were called to serve the church as elders, teachers and pastors. Times have changed. Some of the major North

American denominations now refuse ordination to persons who do not approve of women elders and pastors. It is to these matters that we must turn. In doing so, we need to consider first the practice of the early church and then its teaching. What official roles did women play in the early church, and why?

Women were *prophets*. The daughters of Philip and women at Corinth were prophets (Acts 21:9; 1 Cor. 11:5). The role of a prophet, however, is not a formal institutional role. It is a charismatic gift.

Widows who served well were enrolled on the welfare roll of the church (1 Tim. 5:3–16). These women were apparently not formal representatives of their congregations, but were well respected.

Junias was outstanding among the *apostles* (Rom. 16:7). There is much debate about Junias' gender and the nature of her/his apostleship. Paul's word, *junian*, may be a masculine or a feminine form. Any conclusions about women drawn from this person must, therefore, be tentative.

Paul's comment that she/he is outstanding *among* (*en*) the apostles may mean that she/he is well known *by* the apostles, *or* well known *as* an apostle. In addition, the word 'apostle' may mean someone sent out to represent others in a task of any sort, a missionary sent out by a church or churches, or one on a par with the twelve disciples/apostles. Which is meant in Romans 16:7?

Paul was not in the habit of commending people on the basis of whom they knew. It is not at all likely that he was saying that Junias was highly regarded by the apostles. It is further unlikely that Junias was simply a representative (apostle) of some group for some unidentified task. It is much more likely in the context of Romans 16 that she/he represented a church or churches.

It is inconceivable that Paul was identifying Andronicus and Junias as apostles in the sense that the twelve were apostles. Not only was that number restricted (and thus Paul considered his own apostolate an extraordinary one, 1 Cor. 15:7–9; 2 Cor. 12:11–12; Gal. 1:17, 19), but can we really believe that these two 'outstanding' apostles would be unknown outside this passing greeting, or that

Paul would nestle such a pair in the midst of miscellaneous greetings? It is much more likely that these two were missionaries, fellow workers of Paul as were so many others in Romans 16, and thus apostles in the same sense that Paul and Barnabas were 'apostles' of the church of Antioch (Acts 14:4, 14). In other words, they were sent out by the church to spread the gospel. Romans 16:7, I conclude, tells us about two outstanding missionaries, one of whom may well have been a woman.

Phoebe was a *diakonos* of the church in Cenchreae (Rom. 16:1–2). *Diakonos* means either deacon or servant. If the name in Romans 16:1 were, let us say, Jacob, virtually all commentators would agree that he was an officer and only a few would note the possibility that he was only a servant. Many would note that his activities are precisely those which a deacon would be engaged in. In the absence of other factors, the same would be done for Phoebe. But there *are* other factors which must be looked at before we can decide about Phoebe. Chief among them are passages in Paul's other letters which many feel would prohibit a woman from serving as a deacon.

Women and ministry in the teaching of the apostolic church

One body

The work of Jesus Christ ended divisions among persons. Paul tells us that Christ's death tore down the dividing-wall between Jew and Gentile (Eph. 2:14) and united all kinds of persons in the one body of Christ (1 Cor. 12:12). In this new oneness there is no more Jew or Greek, male and female, slave or free (Gal. 3:28).[8] But unity and oneness are not the same as interchangeability and being identical. Paul both recognized differences between Christians and also insisted that they were one: 'We were all baptized by one Spirit into one body.' 'The body is a unit, though it is made up of many parts; and though its parts

[8] *Cf.* Daphne Key's article in this volume, and J. Hurley, *Man and Woman in Biblical Perspective*, pp. 125–128.

are many, they form one body' (1 Cor. 12:13 and 12; *cf.* also verses 14, 27–30, NIV). How, we must ask, does this work out in the case of men and women in the ministries of the church?

Women and authority
Chapter 2 of 1 Timothy discusses the relation of men and women with respect to formal teaching in the church. Chapter 3 focuses upon the qualifications for persons who will be elders or deacons.

Concerning women and authority Paul said, 'A woman should learn in quietness and full submission. I do not permit a woman to teach or to have authority over a man; she must be silent. For Adam was formed first, then Eve. And Adam was not the one deceived; it was the woman who was deceived and became a sinner' (1 Tim. 2:11–14, NIV).

These verses form the heart of the debate over the ministry of women. They are worthy of close attention.[9]

Verses 11 and 12 address the same situation from two sides. Paul wants women to *learn* quietly and submissively and will not permit them to *teach* authoritatively. The situation in view appears to be formal teaching in the assembly (*cf.* verses 8–10). Christian women were present at worship and learnt from teaching. They were, however, to do so 'quietly'. Paul's actual words do not mean 'with buttoned lips' but have the connotation of learning with a quiet, receptive spirit. Paul will not permit the opposite to take place; he will not allow women to teach or to exercise authority over men. The teaching in view is formal teaching, teaching which comes with disciplinary authority and ought to be quietly received by those under authority. It is easy to see that the opposite of learning quietly and submissively is teaching verbally and with authority.

Paul's language not only qualifies teaching as an exercise of authority, but by means of the 'or' before 'to have authority' also extends his prohibition to other exercises of formal authority. The strength of Paul's feeling can be

[9] *Cf. Man and Woman in Biblical Perspective*, pp. 197–222.

gauged by his verb: *epitrepō*, 'I do not permit. . .'. This verb does not mean 'to advise' or 'to suggest'. It means 'to permit' or 'to allow'. Interestingly, it is the same verb he used in 1 Corinthians 14:34, where he would not permit women to speak in the evaluation of prophetic messages: another speaking situation which involved an exercise of authority.[10]

We sometimes wonder what is meant by 'exercise authority' (*authentein*). The AV translated the word by 'usurp authority'. A close examination of all known uses of this verb made by George Knight[11] reveals that it does not mean wrongful or usurped authority, but rather corresponds simply to the neutral English verb. What Paul forbade was women having and exercising that sort of authority which church members ought to accept quietly and submissively.

It is precisely here that this text speaks to the role of women as elders. The elders were responsible to proclaim faithfully God's truth (2 Tim. 1:13–14; 2:2), to protect the flock of God against false teaching, and to nurture it in its growth in grace (Acts 20:25–31). The writer to the Hebrews calls upon his readers to obey their leaders and to submit to their authority (Heb. 13:17). If *any* role in the church involves authority it is that of the elder. This fact has caused the church to hold, on the basis of 1 Timothy 2:12–15, for nearly two millennia that women are not called to be elders.

It seems to me that the church has been right in its assessment.

Twentieth-century thinkers have asked some new questions about this issue. Could it be that Paul took his position because women were uneducated in those days or because his culture would not have accepted women elders? Are Paul's comments relevant only to his culture and, therefore, not applicable to ours? We might be able to answer these questions if we knew on what basis Paul

[10] *Cf.* Daphne Key's article, and J. Hurley, *Man and Woman in Biblical Perspective*, pp. 185–194.

[11] G. W. Knight, 'AUΘENTEΩ in reference to women in 1 Timothy 2.12', *New Testament Studies* 30, 1984, pp. 143–157.

held the view which he expressed in verses 11 and 12. Our answers lie in verses 13 and 14.

Why women may not exercise authority in the church: an excursus on Paul and Genesis 1 – 3

In support of his position, Paul advanced two considerations: First, that Adam was first formed then Eve, and second, that Adam was not the one deceived, but that the woman, being deceived, became a sinner (1 Tim. 2:13–14).

Does he mean that the mere temporal priority of Adam's formation gave him authority? Why should it? Should the animals, who were formed before Adam, have authority with respect to him? Paul's remark about Adam not being deceived is equally perplexing. Does he mean that women are gullible and men are not? Should women be punished for Eve's failure? Should we follow a rebellious man rather than a deceived woman?

One other question is frequently raised at this point. Does not Genesis 1 teach an equality of the marriage partners? Does not Genesis 3 teach that the subordination of women to men is the result of the fall? If so, should we not see Christ as undoing the effects of the fall, and thereby doing away with inequalities between men and women?

An examination of Genesis 1 – 3 and Paul's use of those chapters will help resolve our questions about his reasoning in 1 Timothy 2 and about the implications of Genesis 1 – 3.[12]

Genesis 1

'God said, "Let us make man in our image, after our likeness; and let them have dominion over [all the creatures of the earth]." So God created man in his own image, in the image of God he created him; male and female he created them' (Gn. 1:26–27).

These two verses make no distinction between the first man and his partner. Both are called to rule over the earth

[12] This treatment of Genesis 1 – 3 has been drastically shortened for space reasons. *Cf.* J. Hurley, *Man and Woman in Biblical Perspective*, pp. 204–220.

and both are made in the image of God. Does this passage show that God's design for human beings includes no distinctions between men and women?

Let us consider the context of the verses to see what is in view. Chapter 1 demonstrates God's lordship and rule over his creation. He commands, and things come to be (verses 3, 5, 9, 14, 20, 24). God, however, is not the only ruler in the chapter. The day and night of the first day are ruled by the sun, moon and stars of the fourth. The sky and seas of the second day are ruled by the birds and fishes of the fifth. The dry land and plants of the third day are ruled over by the animals of the sixth. Over these three pairs of realms and rulers, God places mankind, to rule as God's image. The birds, fishes, animals and people are called upon to multiply and to rule their realms. In each case God is discussing kinds or types of creatures in relation to realms which they rule. The text of Genesis 1 focuses upon relations *between rulers and realms* rather than upon relations within species or kinds of rulers. Genesis 1 does not teach about relations between men and women. The next chapter does.

Genesis 2

This chapter gives account of the creation of Adam and then of Eve to be a fitting helper for him (Gn. 2:7, 18–24). Paul's observation that the man was first formed is certainly correct, but what does it matter?

The Old and New Testament teaching on primogeniture (being born first) helps at this point. Under Old Testament law the first son inherited a 'double portion' of his father's estate (*i.e.* twice what his brothers received), and became head of the household and leader of its worship. With this privilege, however, went the responsibility for the well-being of the widow and any dependants (Dt. 21:15–17; *cf*. Gn. 29:3; 27:19; Lk. 15:11–32; 2 Ki. 2:19).

Paul applies this to Christ, the 'firstborn' over all creation (Col. 1:15–18). Paul is not saying that Christ is the first creation, but that he has the authoritative role of the 'firstborn', 'in everything he [has] the supremacy' (verse 18).

Adam and Eve were not born; they were formed by God. Paul, therefore, says 'Adam was first formed' when he indicates Adam's authoritative role. Paul applied these creational roles in the church.

Genesis 2 reflects the rule of the man over the animals in his naming them (Gn. 2:19–20). For the Hebrew, names are not just identifying vocables, they are statements defining an entity. When God 'makes his name known' it is not the sounds but the corresponding expression of his character which is in view; declaring God's name is acknowledging his deeds or self, not assigning vocables to him (Gn. 16:13). The right to assign a name is the right to exercise authority. This authority is demonstrated when God renames Jacob/Israel or Adam names the animals. It is, therefore, significant that Adam, the first formed, named his wife (Gn. 2:19–23).

Was Paul grasping at straws in 1 Timothy when he related male leadership to the fact that the man was first formed? Our study of primogeniture and naming in Genesis 2 suggests the opposite. The first-formed/born in Genesis exercised authority by naming.

Genesis 3

Paul's second line of argument in 1 Timothy 2 has to do with the woman being deceived and the man not. To see the relevance of this fact, we must look at Genesis 3.

Rabbinic Judaism often viewed the Bible as laying responsibility for the fall at the feet of the woman. Modern chauvinists and some feminist critics have supported this view. Paul did not. In Romans 5:12–21 and 1 Corinthians 15 he blames Adam; it was through the sin of one *man* that sin entered the world.

Some interpreters of 1 Timothy 2 have thought that Paul was saying that all women are gullible and untrustworthy as teachers. His respect for Prisca, wide use of women fellow workers, commendation of the teaching given to Timothy by his mother and grandmother, and instruction that older women should teach the younger, all argue against such a position (Rom. 16:3–4; 2 Tim. 3:15; Tit. 2:3).

It was, however, his view that Eve was deceived (1 Tim. 2:14; 2 Cor. 11:2). The text of Genesis lends support to this contention and offers insight into Paul's point. Genesis 2:15–17 reports that, prior to Eve's formation, God commanded Adam, the first formed, to tend and guard the garden and not to eat of the tree of the knowledge of good and evil. Adam, priest for his family, evidently told God's command to his wife, for Eve was clearly aware of it when she was deceived by the serpent (Gn. 3:2–3).

The serpent is cursed for his deception (verse 14). The man seeks to pass blame off on to the woman whom God had, after all, given to him (verse 12). God will not accept this and curses Adam and the earth for his disobedience (verse 17). Priestly leadership responsibility and rebellion were Adam's; Eve had not been prepared for leadership in this area and was deceived. Paul alludes to these facts in his cryptic remark about her being deceived (1 Tim. 2:14). Eve's curse (Gn. 3:16) is not specifically based on her sin. I suspect this is the first noted consequence of original sin.

Is this culturally relative?

We began this section by asking whether Paul's instructions in 1 Timothy might be irrelevant today because they were designed for a culture which would be offended by women in authority or in which women were uneducated. We can now answer the question.

Paul willingly made accommodations to passing customs in order to win people to Christ ('all things to all men', to win them, 1 Cor. 9:22). He was unwilling to do so in matters of principle. His stance on circumcision and on the inclusion of Gentiles alongside Jews makes that clear. There is no suggestion that his instructions regarding women have anything to do with possible cultural offence. Nor is there any hint that his reasoning was based upon the ignorance of women. His practice of using women as fellow workers, commending Priscilla, recommending that women teach women, and praising Timothy's mother and grandmother for their teaching completely belie this sort of view. There is simply no evidence to support the contention that possible cultural offence or the uneducated status of many women influenced his stance.

Our investigation has found instead that Paul based his position upon the teaching of Genesis 1, 2 and 3 concerning the pre-fall situation of Adam and Eve. He directed that the creational model be implemented in Christ's church in his own day.

What about our day? It seems to me that the creational model is as relevant to our century as it was to Paul's. I have never seen any reasoning which suggested otherwise. *If Paul did not base his conclusions on culturally relative grounds but rather on creational patterns, any suggestion that other conclusions than his should be reached must show why Paul's appeal to creation was relevant for the church in his day but not for the church in ours.* We cannot dismiss Paul's teaching by refuting arguments which he did not advance. We must deal with his actual method of argument, if we are to deal fairly with God's Word.

This last conclusion gains extra weight when we consider that we have found that in each biblical time-period, God appointed some – and only some – of the men to function as leaders of the worshipping community. Adam, the patriarchs, the Aaronic priest and the male teachers of the Pauline churches fall into this pattern. In each period all other men and all women were not called to lead or to discipline in cultic activity. To overthrow this uniform biblical pattern requires clearcut and forceful *biblical* argument. In the absence of such, 1 Timothy 2:11–14 prohibits us from electing women elders in the church.

Elders and deacons in 1 Timothy 3

Husbands of one wife

The third chapter of 1 Timothy lists the high qualifications for elders and deacons, demanding a person whose life will not disgrace the gospel.

It has been observed that the lists demand that elders and deacons be monogamists (literally, one-woman-men), husbands of one wife. From this some deduce that they must be men. This text alone does not require such a conclusion. It would have been unthinkable in that culture for a woman to be married to two men. Polyandry was adultery and a capital offence. Paul would not have to address the issue directly. The expression 'husband of one wife' is, therefore, not relevant to our study.

Women deacons?

The discussion of deacons is particularly interesting because of the mention of a group of women in the midst of the discussion of diaconal qualifications. Are they deacons? Miscellaneous women? Deacons' wives? Elders' and deacons' wives? Paul's word, *gynaikes*, may mean either women or wives. The context must provide our clue to their identity.

The likelihood that they are miscellaneous women is nil. Such a group would not appear in the midst of a discussion of deacons.

It is equally unlikely that the wives of elders *and* deacons would suddenly appear in the middle of a discussion of deacons.

Are they then deacons' wives or themselves deacons? Many translations assume the former and gratuitously supply 'their' before the word *gynaikes*. Paul could have done so, but did not. Paul introduced the elders' children by saying 'having children who . . .' (verse 4). He might have introduced wives by 'having wives who . . .', but did not. His actual construction sets this group of women as a class *parallel to* the elders and the deacons. He said 'elders must be . . . likewise deacons (must be) . . . likewise women (must be). . .'. His mention of deacons and 'women' are clauses without verbs, both presuming the verb of the sentence which mentions the elders. Finally, the list of qualifications for the 'women' is, item for item, parallel to that for the deacons. Only the qualifications for male deacons listed in verse 12 (after the list of requirements for the women) are omitted from the women's list and they are qualifications which would be irrelevant to women.

While it is possible that Paul made no mention of elders' wives and chose to interrupt his discussion of deacons to comment that deacons' wives should have qualifications as high as their husbands', I think it more likely that he was discussing women deacons. Verse 11 is the proper place to list qualifications for women deacons. It places the list of their qualifications directly after the list for the men. And *gynaikes* is the proper term to identify them. This is the case because at that time there was no Greek word for 'deaconess'. It would be coined by the church over a century later. The only term which was available was *diakonos*, a masculine noun which served for either men or women. If Timothy knew of women deacons, it was unnecessary to use the clumsy construction *gynaikes diakonoi* (women who are deacons, a feminine plural followed by a masculine plural) as it would be obvious which women were being mentioned in the middle of a discussion of deacons.

For these reasons I believe that 1 Timothy 3:11 specifically talks of women deacons. I believe as well that Phoebe in Romans 16:1 is a woman deacon from the Cenchreaen church.

Having said this I must comment on the nature of the diaconate and how it relates to teaching and exercising authority in 1 Timothy 2. I understand the New Testament to call for elders, who are responsible for the protection, spiritual growth and discipline of the flock. Deacons are responsible for representing and leading the people of God in the expression of the love of God in-deed. The term 'deacon' means servant, and is exemplified in the services which the 'deacons' of Acts 6 and Phoebe rendered. *As defined* (and I believe this a correct biblical definition of elder and deacon) the office of the deacon does not come within the purview of the prohibition of 1 Timothy 2, because it simply does not involve formal teaching or disciplinary authority. The diaconate is, therefore, not prohibited to women.

In conclusion

We have surveyed the role of women in ministry throughout the Bible. Its pattern is clear and uniform from start to finish. In the broad area of ministry, defined as the service of man and God out of love for God, there is no distinction between men and women. In the particular area of authoritative leadership in the religious community we see a different pattern. In this area God has, *in each period of history*, called out *some* men to lead and to bear the responsibility. His choosing was never based upon a presumed greater personal worth or dignity. In the cases of the patriarchs and the Levites it was not even a matter of particular gifts; it was a matter of order of birth.

God's calling out of certain men is not sexist in contemporary terms. His division has not been: men/women, but rather; certain men/others. Thus it was patriarch/others, Aaronic priest/others, and now is elder/others.

In the New Testament church we found women fully involved in the worship of the community, in the missionary work, in the diaconal meeting of the needs of the people, and in the diaconate itself. Modern churches have often restricted women more than the apostolic church did. Women are not only generally cut off from the diaconate, but are often cut off from missionary labour except as nurses or as school teachers. In congregational life there have arisen numerous activities which are seen as 'men's work' or as 'women's work'. Scripture does not recognize these distinctions.

As far as I can see, Scripture restricts the eldership to certain men with certain gifts and qualifications. Beyond that it knows no official gender distinctions within the organization of the church. I am not addressing the question of marital or social roles at this point. It is our common task to stimulate one another to love and to the fullest possible growth in the Lord. We should grow to the very limits of the freedom to which Christ has set us free. In doing this we may not go beyond what is written; nor may we shrink from declaring the freedom which he declares, so that the body of Christ may fully benefit from godly use of the gifts of all of its members.

Women in the church

Daphne Key

Galatians 3:23–28 · 1 Corinthians 11:1–16 ·
1 Corinthians 14:33–37 · 1 Timothy 2:8–15

For a long time the Bible's teaching on God's order for
men and women was neglected. The rise of the women's
liberation movement, society's concern for women's
rights, legislation for equal opportunity, International
Women's Year and similar developments, have now stimulated the church to re-appraise women's role. Since the
early seventies, a great deal has been written on the
subject. Sadly, the search for biblical principles is sometimes neglected by writers on opposing 'sides', who quote
Bible verses without due regard for their context.

This essay will consider women's contribution to the
ministry of the church. Despite the often heated discussions of the past decade, some local congregations have
changed very little in this respect. Views still range from
the 'hushed-and-hatted' approach at one extreme, to the
liberated approach of licensed female preachers and
pastors at the other.

Dr Jim Hurley's essay has dealt in some detail with
the role of women in the Old Testament, contemporary
Judaism and Hellenism, and has emphasized the revolutionary attitudes of Jesus himself. I would therefore like
to concentrate on the New Testament, and to discuss
particularly passages in the epistles of Paul on which
current debate so often centres.

It is possible that much of our Christian disagreement on this subject arises from confusion about Paul's teaching. On the one hand, some point to Galatians 3:28 and assert the equality of men and women. On the other hand, some conclude, from passages such as 1 Corinthians 14, that women may not speak at all during church services. Neither view does justice to the biblical teaching. Equality does not necessarily mean sameness. And neither, as we will see, must we go along with those who will not even permit women to read from the Scriptures during worship.

We shall examine some of the more controversial Bible passages and try to ascertain what they are really saying.

Galatians 3:23–28

These verses are part of Paul's discussion of the basis on which Christians are accepted by God. The Galatian church was being influenced by Jewish ritualists, who urged a return to circumcision as a ground of acceptance, as though faith in Christ alone were insufficient. In verses 23–29, Paul is saying that in Christ there is no distinction between Jew and Greek; or, for that matter, between man and woman or slave and free. In baptism all demonstrate their faith in Christ and put on his righteousness. Nothing else is necessary. The point of his statement that 'all are one in Christ Jesus' is that there are no degrees of salvation. All the old barriers have been torn down; though all have sinned, all can be restored to a relationship with the Father through the work of the Son. Paul is not discussing roles within the church, but the equality before God of all members of the redeemed community.

This may not seem very revolutionary to us, but when one considers that the average male Jew would have thanked God daily that he had not been born a Gentile, a woman or a slave, it would certainly have sounded very revolutionary to those who wished to impose Jewish regulations on the church of Christ. But such was not to be allowed. There were to be no second-class Christians. And it is very clear from this passage that, in God's eyes,

Jews and Greeks and all men and women are equal.

Equality of status, however, does not necessarily imply equality of role. It is therefore inappropriate to argue from Galatians 3:28 that women may now exercise the same roles as men in the church.

1 Corinthians 11:1-16

This letter was written to a church facing many problems, including that of defining the role of the women members. Much has been written on the meaning of this passage,[1] but space does not permit a discussion of the niceties of the point. What is clear is that the passage in question is saying firstly that there is a created order in relationships, and that that order is 'God – Christ – man – woman' (verse 3); secondly, that women as well as men are expected to participate in prayer and prophecy (verse 5a), but women are to do so in a way that will not make the angels consider that they are stepping outside their God-given role (verse 5b and the rest of the passage).

Let us look at these points more closely. Firstly, *there is a created order in relationships.* Most commentators agree that these relationships do not parallel each other precisely. Paul begins by saying that Christ is the head of every man. He then adds that as God is the head of Christ, so man is the head of woman – a parallel elucidated by Paul in Ephesians 5 with specific reference to marriage. He bases his argument that Christ is the head of woman on the order of creation as we find it in Genesis 2. But he is quick to remind his readers that in the Lord the two are interdependent. God has seen fit to arrange things so that, although man was created first, and woman was created out of man, it is now necessary for man to be born of woman. Within the created order, there is

---

[1] Especially see J. Hurley, *Man and Woman in Biblical Perspective* (IVP, 1981), where he concludes that what Paul is teaching is not that women should be veiled for worship (some translations unhelpfully use the word 'veil' where the original does not), but that their long hair which is their 'pride' should not be cut off in an attempt to be like a man, nor should it be left loose as was the custom of 'loose' women.

interdependence.

Secondly, *Paul assumes that women will pray and prophesy*. He does not disallow the practice. It is a point to be remembered when interpreting his injunction that 'as in all the churches of the saints, the women should keep silence in the churches' (1 Cor. 14:34).[2] A woman is not to display attitudes which could be taken as displacing the headship of man. She must not obliterate the differences between the sexes (in this case, by the way she dresses). It has been suggested that this passage applies only to married women; but as Paul argues from the order of creation, this view is not tenable. Presumably its proponents would not wish to say that only married men sinned in Adam!

1 Corinthians 14:33–37

The context of this passage is that of a church worship service beset with problems. Paul is establishing guidelines for the use of spiritual gifts, 'according to the norm which edifies (verse 26) and according to the rule which is summarized at the end of the chapter, "but let all things be done decently and in order" '.[3] Professor Knight helpfully points out that the words used here of women ('speak' and 'keep silent') are also used of tongue-speakers (verses 27–28) and of prophets (verses 29–30). In both these cases, for one reason or another, people who wish

[2] Concerning prophecy, it seems that confusion often arises over the question of women preaching in church because it is not allowed that prophecy can still be an 'inspired revelation' (as in 1 Cor. 14); in this view, all prophecy is seen in terms of the ministry of the Word from the pulpit. To understand prophecy in that light provides a reason for disregarding Paul's teaching in 1 Timothy 2, and concluding that women may preach. There would however seem to be no grounds given in the New Testament for a merging of the gifts of prophecy and preaching. Thus – to clarify – I do not, when using the term 'prophecy', understand 'preaching', but 'the inspired utterance of a message from God with direct application to a specific situation'.

[3] G. W. Knight, *The New Testament Teaching on the Role Relationship of Male and Female*: with Special Reference to the Teaching Functions of the Church.

to participate in worship are told to be silent; not for all time, but in specific circumstances. What then do the words mean in the present context?

The various interpretations of the passage may be summarized as follows:

a. Paul is saying that women should not teach men (*cf.* 1 Tim. 2:11ff.) or ask questions during worship;

b. Because Paul enjoins women to be 'subordinate even as the law says', and as the 'law' is now superseded, the passage is of no significance in the debate;

c. The passage is talking about judging prophecy. A woman who participated would thereby be 'in authority' over man, and this would flout the creation order about which Paul has already written;

d. The passage teaches that women should be silent at all times during worship;

e. The passage is not normative, as it refers to a situation which hardly ever occurs today.

Three chapters earlier in the epistle, Paul referred to women praying and prophesying in the context of worship, and he did not appear to condemn the practice. He cannot therefore be forbidding women to speak at all in worship.

Perhaps our English translations are partly to blame for the confusion. The RSV and NIV, among others, begin a new paragraph with verse 33b, thereby separating the passage about women from the one about judging the prophets. If, however, verses 26–40 are read as a single paragraph, the sense of the passage is greatly clarified. It seems (verse 33) that there is confusion in the church. Everyone is so keen to have their say that tongue-speaking and prophecy have become completely unruly; and it is with this problem that the chapter deals (*cf.* verses 1–5, and also verses 39–40). It is in this context that Paul addresses women. His concern is that they should be 'subordinate' (verse 34), that they should realize that God's Word did not originate with them (verse 36). This would imply that Paul's theme here is that women should not step outside their place in the created order (*cf.* 1 Cor. 11 for a different issue).

In verse 28 tongue-speakers are told to be silent if there is no interpretation. And in verse 30, prophets are told that if a revelation is made to another, the first is to be silent. Then in verse 34 we find that women too are to keep silent. It would seem natural to infer that, as in the other two cases, this is a particular command, not a general one. It has been suggested that in this case the particular situation is the weighing or judging of a prophecy or revelation, and this too would seem to be a natural interpretation. Perhaps the women were butting in with possible interpretations, or querying interpretations already given. Paul is saying that it is not for the women to judge; but, if they have any queries, let them sort them out at home with their husbands.

It has sometimes been asked, how would this ruling apply to single women? But it cannot be permissible for any woman to step outside the created order that was part of the world even before the fall. Paul instructs women to resolve their queries with their own husbands, because in his society adult women were usually married.

This passage aims to change a situation of chaos and disorder into one of order, harmony and edification, with women assuming their rightful place within God's created structures. It does not teach that women must be silent in church at all times.

1 Timothy 2:8–15

This is another passage illustrating Paul's concern that the church should be at peace and that it should be built up in the faith. Here, he calls women to demonstrate the reality of their faith by modest dress and a life of 'good deeds, as befits women who profess religion' (verse 10).

Paul then goes on to deal with the place of women in two areas of the church's life. In verse 11, he repeats to the church at Ephesus what he has already said to the church at Corinth: women should learn 'with all submissiveness', that is, within their place in God's created order. Verses 12–14, however, relate this to a different area, that of 'teaching' and 'having authority over men'.

Firstly, Paul says 'I permit no woman to teach'. From the context, it seems that Paul has the mixed congregation of the church in mind. In Titus 2:3–5 he does encourage older women to teach younger women by word and by example, in matters relating, interestingly enough, not to doctrine but to the practical outworking of the Christian faith in the home and in society. In this letter to Timothy, Paul is saying that women are not to teach the church congregation as a whole. Since 'to teach' translates a Greek present infinitive, what is implied is 'regular teaching'. In our culture, this perhaps applies most directly to teaching 'occasions' such as Sunday worship, which are a regular feature of the church's life.

Many still find this prohibition uncomfortable and try to minimize its contemporary relevance, by saying that Paul, conditioned by his own culture, was simply reflecting the typical outlook of Jewish Christian males of the period. Others argue that it applies only to married women, or that it applies primarily to the family and only indirectly to the church, or that it is of no great importance in any case, as it is only Paul's opinion – '*I* do not permit.'

In verses 13–14 Paul presents the basis for his teaching. He appeals not to Graeco-Roman culture, nor even to the Mosaic law, but to creation principles. He has, as we have already seen, touched upon this in 1 Corinthians; and here again we find him applying pre-fall principles to the Kingdom of God. Adam, he points out, was formed first; thus Paul implies everything that we have already noted about the man's headship.[4] He also remarks upon the deception of Eve. Her sin, he maintains, lay in the fact that she allowed herself to be deceived. Adam's was straightforward, deliberate disobedience, as shown in Genesis 2 and 3. The woman, however, was beguiled into disobeying. Paul appears to be saying that woman's senses and feeling are in the nature of things likely to render her more susceptible than man to deception by externals; and this is why she ought not to teach man.

---

[4] *Cf.* the section 'Paul on Genesis 1 – 3' in J. Hurley's contribution to this volume (pp. 133–136).

Paul's argument, then, is really two arguments. Firstly, the argument from creation order: woman should not teach man. Secondly, the argument from man's and woman's natures: woman is the more easily led astray. He sees no need to argue the matter further. Nor can we protest that these arguments apply only to Paul's cultural context, since they are based on principles which are authoritative for all time. They are as binding in the last decades of the twentieth century as they were in the last decades of the first.

Paul goes on to say that he permits no woman to have authority over man. In this passage, and in 1 Corinthians 14, we see two specific outworkings of this prohibition. From them we may conclude that although a woman may participate in worship she may not place herself in a position of authority over men – as would certainly be the case should she become involved in the regular teaching ministry or in judging prophecy.

Joyce Baldwin argues that Paul is forbidding only married women to teach.[5] But this interpretation does not bear scrutiny. Although the words translated 'man' and 'woman' could be translated also as 'husband' and 'wife', Genesis 2 (the source of Paul's teaching) indicates that this order in man/woman relationships existed even before the man and woman cleaved to each other and became one flesh.[6] Paul's teaching applies to women irrespective of their marital status.

How then can we define the areas of ministry open to women within the church? Perhaps we can find help by considering the roles adopted by some of the women in the Bible.

The Bible certainly leaves us in no doubt that God regarded women highly. The Saviour of mankind was

[5] Joyce Baldwin, *Women Likewise* (Falcon, 1973).
[6] Not only was man created before woman, but the man named the woman, an act which in itself expressed headship. The Lord named the man *ish*; the man named the woman *ishshah*. The act, as well as expressing headship, also expresses the complementary aspect of the relationship.

born of a woman. Women were the first witnesses of the resurrection, the event at the core of the Christian faith. At times God chose to intervene in the history of Israel through the agency of a woman. Deborah and Esther are prime examples; Deborah, as prophetess and civil judge, held a position of very great responsibility in Israel.[7]

At the birth of the church women devoted themselves to prayer alongside men (Acts 1:13–14). There is no reason to suppose that they were not in the group upon which the Spirit descended, especially in view of Peter's quotation from Joel: 'Yea, and on my menservants and my maidservants in those days I will pour out my Spirit, and they shall prophesy. . . .' (Acts 2:18). Women presumably were also among those who devoted themselves to the apostles' teaching, fellowship, prayer and the breaking of bread (Acts 2:42). The new Christian community no longer scorned the idea that women were capable of being taught, as had been the case in Jewish congregations.

Then there are individuals such as Tabitha (Acts 9:36ff.), who was 'full of good works and acts of charity', using her talents to provide her friends with clothes. There was Mary the mother of John Mark (Acts 12:12f.) who opened her home for the church's use. Lydia, a business woman and the first Macedonian convert, was eager to receive the Lord Jesus Christ and offered Paul hospitality during his stay there. Priscilla, with her husband Aquila, became a great friend and co-worker with Paul, and the couple together helped Apollos to understand the faith. Together they risked their lives for Paul's sake (Rom. 16:3), and had a 'church in their house' (1 Cor. 16:19). From Priscilla alone, we could gather that there was great scope for women's ministry in the church.

In his greetings to the church at Rome, Paul mentions a woman deacon:

> I commend to you . . . Phoebe, a deaconess of the church at Cenchreae, that you may receive her in the Lord as befits the saints, and help her in whatever she

[7] See J. Hurley, *Man and Woman in Biblical Perspective*, for further discussion of this point.

may require from you, for she has been a helper of
many and of myself as well (Rom. 16:1).

Here was a woman who helped Paul and held office in
the church at Cenchreae. But what exactly did the office
of deacon entail in Paul's day? Does this verse support the
idea of women having 'authority' in the church? It may
help to consider Acts 6, where a group (here, of men) is
first appointed to 'serve'. The noun 'deacon' comes from
the Greek *diakoneō*, which means 'to serve'. The apostles
were having difficulty over practical arrangements in the
church. Rather than give up the preaching of the Word to
deal with them, they appointed seven men to 'serve at
tables', freeing the apostles themselves for teaching and
prayer.

1 Timothy 3:1–13 lists qualities expected of those
holding office in the church. Deacons are to be 'serious,
not double-tongued, not addicted to much wine, not
greedy for gain; they must hold the mystery of the faith
with a clear conscience'. These characteristics would fit
somebody charged with practical responsibility in the
church. In 1 Timothy 3:11 the phrase sometimes rendered
'the women' or 'their wives' (that is, of the male deacons)
could be translated 'the deaconesses'. This is not necessarily the correct interpretation, but it would certainly
seem the most natural in the context. It is just possible
that 'the women' refers to the deacons' wives, as translated
by the NIV; but there is no possessive pronoun in the
Greek, and as we know of at least one woman deacon
(Phoebe) it seems most likely that in 1 Timothy 3:11 Paul
is referring to the sphere of service of the women who
were also appointed deacons. We may also note that there
is no female equivalent of the teaching elder of 1 Timothy
3:1–7.

What New Testament principles, then, can we apply to
our own church situations? There are still many evangelical Christian churches where women are forbidden to
speak at all in worship. This is surely unscriptural. Women
certainly need to learn to rejoice in their womanhood and
in its distinctiveness, and to accept joyfully their God-

given attributes. As Gladys Hunt says,[8]

> Do not let others poison your joy in being female.
> The possibilities inherent in being made woman are
> as creative as the God who made us. And there is
> great dignity in his design.

But it is very hard not to allow that joy in one's sexuality
to be poisoned, when culture and convenience colour a
church's attitude to its women. Despite all this, our
theology is not to be born out of experience, socially
conditioned or religiously provoked, but out of the search
for biblical foundations. Women should be allowed to
participate together with the men in prayer and prophecy,
worship, pastoral care and counselling, hospitality, evangelism and follow-up. Men and women, as we saw from
Genesis 1:28, were made to complement each other and
to work together, provided that they maintain their God-
given differences and that the woman does not seek to
usurp the man's headship.

Some may be wondering how woman can be regarded
as man's equal while certain areas of ministry are closed
to her. In our society women now (at least in theory) have
equal rights. Should not the church, far from restricting
the activities of women, be taking the lead in these
developments?

Again I would emphasize that the Bible rules out any
notion of women as 'second-class citizens', and stresses
the equality of men and women in their relationship with
God through Christ. Yet it teaches that there is a
functional difference between the sexes in the life of the
church. It is inadmissible to formulate doctrine on the
basis of developments in society, supported by Bible verses
wrested from their context.

Finally, any discussion of the role of women in the
church poses questions about the role of the men. If
women are seeking more masculine roles in the church's
life, is it because so many Christian men have lost their
dynamism and are abdicating *their* God-given responsi-

[8] Gladys Hunt, *MS Means Myself.*

151

bility? Does God really call more women than men to the mission field? Perhaps the men too should be rediscovering their God-given role within the church, and asking themselves how far they are assuming the responsibilities it involves.

Part of the problem arises from the tension between the fallen world in which we live, and the beginnings of God's restorative work in us. We long for the relationships broken at the fall to be healed – for male domination of women (*cf*. Gn. 3:16) to be eradicated and replaced by loving equality. But our ideal runs the risk of distortion when we forget to find its true shape in the Bible. We all need to try to break loose from our prejudices, and to let the Book that speaks for itself, speak.

Response to James Hurley and Daphne Key

I. Howard Marshall

I can comment on these two essays together, since they are very largely in agreement. I do wonder whether Daphne Key should have felt it right, on her premises, to write a piece of teaching that may well be read by men, still less to have taken part in a symposium in which Jim Hurley and I are under the authority of the Editor! However, I am very much in agreement with her comment that the concept of ministry needs re-examination. The following points seem to me to require discussion.

1. I question whether, in the end, Jim Hurley really does justice to *Priscilla*, whose teaching ministry plainly extended to men as well as to women. It is a question of how one harmonizes the prohibition in 1 Timothy 2 with the implicit principles elsewhere in the New Testament. I am dubious about an interpretation which would prevent Priscilla doing now what she clearly did do then.

2. Jim appears to draw *a distinction between 'formal teaching in the assembly' and informal teaching*. I cannot find this distinction in the New Testament and I do not think it is valid; it simply will not do to suggest that the teaching given by Priscilla to Apollos, a future leader in the church, was somehow informal.

3. I suspect that we all need to clarify what we mean by *'authority' and 'leadership'*. 'Leader' is a vague term in

the New Testament, and seems to refer to anybody who, as we say, 'takes the lead' in doing things in church. Such people were to be respected for their work's sake, but were to act as humble servants of the church. Thus they exercised some 'authority', and I cannot see that a prophetess, speaking in the name of the Lord, or a deacon (male or female), was not to some extent functioning as a leader with authority.

4. It can too easily be assumed that the elders and the deacons of the Pastoral Epistles correspond fairly exactly to the elders (including ministers) and deacons in the church today. In fact, *we know very little indeed about the precise functions of elders and deacons in New Testament times.* (*Cf.* 1 Timothy 5:17; did all elders teach?) The similarity between the qualifications for elders and those of deacons is interesting (including that of having the ability to exercise some kind of authority: 1 Timothy 3:4f., 12). One must remember, too, that our modern concept of ordination to '*the* ministry' is not found in the New Testament, where laying on of hands was practised on occasion as a commissioning for various kinds of ministries. (The concept of priesthood is frankly irrelevant, since in the New Testament the priesthood of *all believers* and not merely of *some men* is the appointed pattern in the new creation.)

5. The real bone of contention is the phrase '*to have authority*' in 1 Timothy 2:12. If the basic idea of ministry is humble service, then the prohibition is against women teaching in an authoritative way that would go against the biblical principles of the 'headship' of man in creation and the equality of man and woman in the new creation. The force of 1 Timothy 2:12 is to warn against the temptation to take part in ministry from fallen, sinful motives.

In the eighteenth century, John Wesley was horrified by observing a young man actually preaching without having been ordained. His wise mother (!) advised, 'Take care what you do with respect to that young man, for he is as surely called by God to preach as you are. Examine what have been the fruits of his preaching, and hear him also yourself.' We would do well to beware of prejudice. What matters in the end is the encouragement of sound biblical teaching in the church, and this is more important than debates about which sound Christians are not eligible to provide such teaching.

Response to James Hurley and Daphne Key

Joyce Baldwin

In the short space allowed for this response my hope is to comment on the use made in the New Testament epistles of Genesis 1 – 3, and in particular on the assumption made by Jim Hurley concerning the status of what he refers to as 'creational patterns'. His use of Genesis conflicts with the argument I will propose, that Christ's work of regeneration overrides the results of the fall and tends towards 'Paradise Regained'.

In all the evidence he marshals from the Old Testament, the Gospels and Acts, Jim nowhere quotes any place where the principle behind the so-called 'creational pattern' or 'creation model', of which he speaks, is formulated. There is circumstantial evidence to show that women were not often in positions of authority, but sometimes they were; and this nowhere appears as a subject for the strictures of any prophet. This one would expect to find if his claims for the 'creational pattern' were as conclusive as he suggests. Where indeed was it set out so that all could learn to obey it? The reference in 1 Corinthians 14:34 to 'as even the law says' raises a problem; Genesis 3:16 hardly suits the context, and moreover, as I will argue, though it is part of the *Torah*, it is not prescriptive. The law of which Paul was speaking was almost certainly the oral teaching of his day. Not one of the Old Testament writers appears to have been aware of this law, and Jesus certainly makes no reference to it. Did the true meaning of Genesis 1 – 3 have to wait until late in Paul's ministry to be revealed to the world, even though its truth applied to half of humanity? The suggestion is too fantastic to take seriously. Yet this is what we are being asked to believe.

In the Bible we find certain social structures, but they are incidental to its main message. Its patriarchal organization is not part of the gospel, to be imposed on all believers. Indeed such a task would not prove possible in the Christian world mission. It is clear from the Gospels and Acts that women played a leading role in the early decades of the church's life. Indeed there is evidence that the admission of women and slaves to Christian society interfered with the social structure of Graeco-Roman life almost from the beginning, and there arose a need to divert away from the church the attention of a critical and persecuting world. In the process some of the more revolutionary implications of the faith were played down, as in 1 Corinthians and 1 Timothy.

I am not convinced that the truth of the New Testament texts in question is served by taking them legalistically. Even those who so interpret them do not apply them rigorously across the board. The reason is not far to seek: they do not belong to 'our world'. We need to understand more fully their total context and why the writer wrote as he did. Until that condition is fulfilled, we are not in any position to build on these passages a theological argument, especially one of such magnitude.

Women's ministry: a new look at the biblical texts

Joyce Baldwin

First-century Jewish legalism · Jesus and the letter of the law: an illustration · Consequences of the fall: Genesis 3 · A helper suitable for the man: Genesis 2 · Is there a 'creation ordinance'?: Genesis 1 · A matter of priorities

First-century Jewish legalism

The Jew of the first century BC was familiar with the idea that in the sphere of worship women were in a different category from men, and were strictly limited as to what was permitted to them. Somewhat to our surprise in view of these restrictions, the prophetess Anna 'did not depart from the temple, worshipping with fasting and prayer night and day' (Lk. 2:37). The crown of her ministry was to speak about the child Jesus to all who were waiting for God to set Jerusalem free.

From the beginning of the life of Jesus on earth, both men and women were fully involved. Both Mary and Zechariah contributed their songs to Scripture, both Simeon and Anna had the spiritual perception to recognize the Christ, both Joseph and Mary made a home for him, and to Mary was given the supreme privilege of bearing and nurturing him. Between these events and the legalism of official religion there could scarcely have been a greater contrast. Officially Anna and Mary were restricted, like all Jewish women, to the outermost Jewish court; Jewish laymen were barred from the sanctuary, which was entered only by priests and Levites as they went about their duties. Under the old covenant the way into the holiest of all was not open, and even Jesus was confined to the outer courts of the temple.

No such distinction between men and women at worship had been allowed for in the original design of the tabernacle as it was specified in Exodus 25 – 40, and nowhere in the Old Testament (as opposed to Judaism) is the original design of the temple modified to restrict access by women. It was during the three centuries before the coming of Jesus that new emphasis was placed on exclusiveness, and increased regulations restricted and impeded an earlier freedom in many aspects of life. The lengths to which Jewish leaders were prepared to go have been adequately illustrated by Dr Jim Hurley, and the Gospels present in some detail the conflict that arose between Jesus and the Jewish teachers, whose devotion to the letter of the law frequently caused them to mistake its intention. A tight network of convention characterized Jewish culture and, where Jewish converts predominated, tended to be carried over into the churches. Especially was this the case in the matter of relationships between the sexes, and of propriety in women's dress and hair-styles. Christian freedom could not go beyond what was generally acceptable, with the result that concessions were made to Jewish Christians and their scruples, for instance at the Jerusalem conference (Acts 15). The conservatism of the Jerusalem church which Paul constantly needed to conciliate may well have exceeded in some respects the demands of the Torah and the Prophets.

It is clear from the narrative of the Old Testament that God revealed himself to both men and women. The Egyptian Hagar is a particularly striking example early on in the story (Gn. 16:7–12; 21:17f.), and 'there was no lack of women who acted independently: Rebecca, Deborah, Jael, Abigail, and a whole series of such characters. There may be legal restraint, and yet in daily life complete freedom of action; on all sides we see the Hebrew woman enjoying this freedom.'[1] That this freedom gradu-

---

[1] Ludwig Köhler, *Hebrew Man*, Eng. trans. Peter Ackroyd (SCM Press, 1956), p. 85.

ally became eroded, as the lawyers imposed on society an increasing rigidity, can scarcely be doubted.

The covenant law itself did not as a matter of fact differentiate between what was required of a man as opposed to what was required of a woman, unless, in the fourth commandment, 'you or your son or your daughter, your manservant, or your maidservant . . .' is interpreted to mean 'everyone in the family and farm except your wife'.[2] I cannot remember any teacher or preacher making such a distinction, nor can I believe that it is implied by the wording. True, the masculine form is used; but this was by convention understood to include the feminine, and in any case the covenant was made with 'all the people'. Thus the text supports the thesis that all were expected to keep the covenant law. The question was, what behaviour would guarantee the keeping of the law so that God's wrath would never again bring disaster on the nation?

This kind of consideration lay behind the many prohibitions that regulated Jewish life in the time of Jesus, and to these he generally submitted. But he bequeathed to the church his own interpretation of the law, which quite transformed it.

Jesus and the letter of the law: an illustration

The point at issue may best be made by taking as an example the fourth commandment, to which we have already referred. The church may still not be clear as to what should or should not be permitted on a Sunday, but at least it is agreed that the first and not the seventh day of the week is appropriate for the Christian's day of rest and worship. This is different from the law of Moses and from the practice of Jesus, and therefore demonstrates the radical nature of the church, the new community in Christ. Nothing was quite the same after his coming, and it was this that offended the Jews. What is of importance for our

[2] A. C. Phillips, *Ancient Israel's Criminal Law* (Blackwell, 1970), pp. 67, 71f.

subject is to understand how the work of Christ made a difference to the place of women in the church; but a short examination of the teaching of Jesus on the sabbath law shows how he used the Scriptures to disagree with his hearers.

Jesus was drawn into controversy on the subject of the sabbath because on one occasion his disciples plucked, rubbed and ate grain on the sabbath day (Mt. 12:1–7; Mk. 2:23–28; Lk. 6:1–5); according to the Pharisees, this was not lawful. In the Matthean account Jesus makes reference to three passages in the Old Testament as he expounds the Scriptures on the subject.

The first (1 Sa. 21:1–6) recounts David's emergency visit to the house of God when he was on the run from Saul. Because he and his men were desperately hungry, he was given the bread from the holy place, though it was not lawful for them to eat it because they were not priests. The inference seems to be that the need to save life took precedence over other laws. Perhaps Jesus also took for granted, as his contemporaries would have done, the right of David to override the law. A greater than David was among them.

The second reference is to Numbers 28:9–10, where the law specified the offerings to be made on the sabbath. For the priests, obedience involved work; but the rabbis decreed that temple service took precedence over the sabbath law. A greater than the temple was here.

The last reference, to Hosea 6:6, taught that there was something more important than sacrifice, namely covenant loyalty (Hebrew *ḥesed*) to the Lord. According to Jesus, if they had known the meaning of that saying these accusers would not have condemned the guiltless. Though in the eyes of some the disciples had broken the law, Jesus cleared them of guilt by showing that in the light of more important principles the lesser law had to give way. He, the Lord of the sabbath, went on to demonstrate that it is lawful to do good on the sabbath day (Mt. 12:9–13). While Jesus did his good work his accusers planned his murder, convinced that they had the Word of God on their side.

This is an uncomfortable sequence of events for those who are sensitive over the letter of the law. True, Jesus avoided giving unnecessary cause for offence, but when challenged by acute human need no law – not even one of the Ten Commandments – could forbid his loving act. Of course his contemporaries had a blind spot in this matter. God's law and God's Son were never at odds. When the Holy Spirit ushered in the new order it was the first day of the week that distinguished the church from the old order, for Jesus was the fulfiller of the law and its interpreter.

To return to our topic. Even if there had been a law which said that women were to be banned from all participation in worship (which of course there was not) it would have had to be reviewed in the light of the work of Christ. For that reason arguments against women's ministry which are based on the all-male levitical priesthood, or even on the fact that Jesus appointed only men as his apostles, lack cogency because they are arguments from the old order, on a par with the appeal of certain sects that the church should still observe the seventh day. The old order had passed away and all had become new.

Consequences of the fall: Genesis 3

Despite the fact that the Mosaic law does not prescribe an order for the sexes, it will be argued by some that Scripture ordains such an order nevertheless. When the Lord God says to the woman 'your desire shall be for your husband, and he shall rule over you' (Gn. 3:16), these words are said to imply an order ordained by God for all time. 'God brings structure into the primary relationship', says Francis Schaeffer.[3] By the primary relationship he means the man/woman relationship, and not just the marriage relationship. 'It is not simply because man is stronger that he is to have dominion (that's the argument of the Marquis de Sade). But rather he is to

[3] F. A. Schaeffer, *Genesis in Space and Time: the Flow of Biblical History* (Hodder and Stoughton, 1973), p. 93.

have dominion because God gives this as structure in the midst of a fallen world.'[4] By this interpretation the man is not only permitted to 'rule', but is actually *commanded* to dominate his wife and other female dependents. Can this be the meaning of Genesis 3:16? Is the last clause, 'he shall rule over you', to be taken as an imperative or as a simple future? We shall look first at the Hebrew and various English translations of it, in order to establish the linguistic force of the verb. We shall then see how some representative commentators have interpreted the sense. Finally the likely meaning will be assessed.

The Hebrew verb, like others in the passage, is future in meaning, despite the 'shall' of the AV, RV and RSV. The standard English future is used in the more recent translations, *e.g.* GNB: 'you will be subject to him'; NIV: 'he will rule over you'; though NEB retains the older form, 'and he shall be your master'. Had the writer of Genesis intended to propound a law he could have used the imperative form, such as occurs in the divine fiats of Genesis 1, thus avoiding any ambiguity. The fact that he does not do so but chooses rather the future tense makes it unlikely that he was propounding a law. Ambiguity in the English translations has not helped expositors to understand the meaning.[5]

A century ago, when the subject of women's ministry and the relationship between men and women was less of a burning issue, Delitzsch wrote on the latter part of Genesis 3:16:

> The woman will henceforth involuntarily follow the leading of the man, and be subject even against her will to his dominion. The subordination of the woman to the man was intended from the beginning; but now that the harmony of their mutual wills in God is destroyed, this subordination becomes subjection. The man may command as master, and the woman is bound externally and internally to obey. That slavish subjection of the woman to the man which was customary in the ancient world, and still is

---

[4] *Ibid.*, p. 94.
[5] *Cf.* Luther, *'und er soll dein Herr sein'* (he is to be your master).

in the East, and which revealed religion has gradually made more tolerable and consistent with her human dignity, is the result of sin.'[6]

Delitzsch would evidently not agree with Schaeffer's interpretation of these words, regarding woman's subjection, as a divine law. Early this century Skinner wrote that the pains of childbirth and the desire which makes woman the willing slave of the man impressed the ancient world as unnatural and mysterious.

> The idea of tyrannous exercise of power does not lie in the verb; but it means that the woman is wholly subject to the man, and so liable to the arbitrary treatment sanctioned by the marriage customs of the east. It is noteworthy that to the writer this is not the ideal relation of the sexes (*cf.* 2:18, 23).[7]

The last point is particularly telling: in Skinner's view human aspirations are beyond man's grasp; he can envisage possibilities which are not fulfilled; far from obeying a divine law in dominating his wife, he senses that he should be loving her. Writing within the same decade Driver also sees here the reflection of the oppressed condition of woman in antiquity, 'when she was often not more than the slave of her husband, and was liable to be treated by him with great arbitrariness'.[8]

Among more recent commentators none is more distinguished than Cassuto. On the text before us he writes,

> Measure for measure: you influenced your husband and caused him to do what you wished; henceforth, you and your female descendants will be subservient to your husbands. You will yearn for them, but they will be heads of the families, and will rule over you.[9]

[6] F. Delitzsch, *Commentary on Genesis* (T. & T. Clark, 1888), p. 166.

[7] J. Skinner, *A Critical and Exegetical Commentary on Genesis* (T. & T. Clark, 1910), pp. 82f.

[8] S. R. Driver, *The Book of Genesis* (Methuen, 1904), p. 49.

[9] U. Cassuto, *A Commentary on the Book of Genesis Part I, From Adam to Noah* (Magnes Press, Jerusalem, ET 1961), pp. 165f.

Like the older commentators this outstanding Hebrew scholar saw the dominion of the man as the outcome of sin's entrance into the world, and not as a law representing God's original intention for the human race.

The consensus of these commentary writers, taken together with the meaning of the Hebrew construction, supports the view that woman's subservience is a consequence of the fall into sin. But Christ died to reverse the deadly effects of Adam's fall, and in Christ there is to be mutual submission (Eph. 5:21). In short, Genesis 3:16 is not a verse on which a valid justification of male dominance can be based, any more than it would support the necessity of difficult and painful childbirth.

What then of the opposing arguments based on Genesis 3? It is sometimes assumed, for example, that when Paul in 1 Corinthians 14:34 refers to 'the law' he has Genesis 3:16 in mind, but this is by no means certain. Only because no other passage in the Old Testament says anything of the sort is this verse implicated, for the allusion is entirely vague. Paul is much more likely to be referring to the Jewish law of his day: 'The women should keep quiet in the meetings. They are not allowed to speak; as the Jewish Law says, they must not be in charge' (GNB). Current practice was adequate support for his point. Paul was, after all, writing a letter to his contemporaries, using language and allusions which they would appreciate. If a rabbinic argument suited his purpose Paul felt free to use it. The thrust of this part of his letter was to end the disorderly worship of the Corinthian church, and his argument from Jewish practice needs to be seen in context, and not made a generalization for all time.

Two other arguments may be considered here. Firstly, Dr Hurley has attached considerable importance to the naming of the animals by Adam (Gn. 2:19–20): 'The right to assign a name is the right to exercise authority' (p. 135). But in the Bible the privilege of naming is not by any means always that of the husband, as the book of Ruth plainly shows: 'the women of the neighbourhood gave him a name' (Ru. 4:17). Indeed the Old Testament mentions forty-six cases of naming, of which twenty-eight are by the mother and eighteen by the father.[10] Thus if the argument is valid it supports at least equal authority for the wife as for the husband.

Secondly, while on the subject of laws we may look briefly at Deuteronomy 21:15–17, the law of primogeniture which granted special status, responsibility and reward to the eldest son. Such a privilege is assigned to Jesus when he is figuratively described as 'first-born of all creation' (Col. 1:15–18). Yet God reserved the right to choose Jacob rather than Esau, and to entrust his Son not to the tribe of Reuben the firstborn, but to that of Judah. Similarly he sometimes chose women to take responsibility in particular situations, even in Old Testament times, and still does so today.

A helper suitable for the man: Genesis 2

The second chapter of Genesis is referred to several times in the New Testament to illustrate the relationship between the sexes, and it would be difficult to overestimate its importance, though the exact force of the references is sometimes far from clear. The well-known story of creation, in which the Lord God makes man from the dust of the earth and breathes into him the breath of life, depicts him as the one for whom the garden of Eden was planted and irrigated. The Lord God also intended to provide him with a helper (Hebrew *'ēzer*). The word is most often used in the Old Testament of the Lord who helps and delivers his people (*cf. Ebenezer* ['stone of help']; *Hitherto the Lord has helped us*, 1 Sa. 7:12), and is therefore far from implying subservience. This helper would be a true partner, able to communicate with him at every level. As the man named the various creatures and noted that not one of them lacked a mate, there built up within him a great longing which corresponded with the very gift the Lord was to make. From his very bone and flesh his counterpart was formed.

Just as the rib is found at the side of the man and is

[10] L. Köhler, *Hebrew Man*, p. 63 footnote.

attached to him, even so the good wife, the *rib* of her husband, stands at his side to be his helper-counterpart, and her soul is bound up with his.[11]

This description matches the aspirations of a girl when she marries. She wants a total relationship which will grow and deepen and make her life meaningful. Similarly when the Lord God brought her to the man he responded with delight. She was the one for whom he had been longing, and in whom he could find fulfilment of his personality because she could reciprocate his affection and contribute her gifts to their mutual life task.

There seems to be a kind of memory that marriage should be like this. The human ideal is certainly not a relationship in which one partner dominates the other, but rather a mutually satisfying partnership in which each delights to serve the other. The discrepancy which so often exists between hope and fulfilment in marriage (and the correspondence is never perfect) is one gauge of the disruption caused by sin.

The question may well be asked whether this chapter, which seems to be all about marriage, has any relevance to the subject of women's ministry. In other words, does it have relevance for the single people in society as well as for the married couple, and for relationships within society as a whole? A number of writers imply that it has. Woman was made for man, they say, plucking out of context a few words from Paul in 1 Corinthians 11:9, and therefore it is her role, whether married or not, to serve men. (An interpretation of the 'helper' of Gn. 2:18 seems to creep in here.) Secretarial work and nursing fulfil this role ideally; teaching less so, because it involves a certain degree of authority. Ministry within the church permits a woman to fulfil her God-given role so long as she is under the authority of a man. Opinions differ among those who take this line as to whether she should be permitted a ministry of both word and sacraments, or whether she should be mainly the pastoral visitor. In practice churches rarely find they can support a full-time pastoral visitor,

[11] U. Cassuto, *op. cit.*, p. 124.

and require each member of the staff to participate fully in all that has to be done, so the question is largely academic.

Those who think in this way imply that all women should marry. This is their calling *par excellence*, and since the duties of a wife and mother require all her gifts, she should not take on a full-time role in the church's ministry. Now it is true that the Old Testament presupposes that marriage will be the norm.

> In Jewish thought, as a matter of fact, the man who remained unmarried was really an incomplete and unfinished man; he was like the Adam of the creation story who found no helper suitable for him. And the woman who did not have a husband was simply disgraced.[12]

Jewett goes on to make a most important point concerning the 'absorbing preoccupation of the Old Testament with marriage and the family'. He thinks it arises out of the old covenant promise of a seed, in whom all the nations of the earth were to be blessed. But once the seed of Abraham had come (Gal. 3:16) the situation changed, and this fulfilment of the Old Testament promise in Christ brings the subject of marriage into a new focus.

In the Christian era marriage remained the norm for most people, of course; but there came into play in the New Testament an additional factor, the pre-eminent claims of Christ. Jesus spoke of 'eunuchs who have made themselves eunuchs for the sake of the kingdom of heaven' (Mt. 19:12), and of disciples who left 'house or wife or brothers or parents or children, for the sake of the kingdom of God' (Lk. 18:29). Such renunciation of life's responsibilities and commitments is conceivable only in the face of the even greater claims of the kingdom of God. Paul realized that his travels as an apostle to the Gentiles, with all the rigours and attacks he had to suffer, required of him celibacy, though he had the right to the company of a wife. These were practical arguments, relevant also

---

[12] Paul K. Jewett, *Man as Male and Female* (Eerdmans, Grand Rapids, 1975), p. 121.

to the church in Corinth in view of pending calamities (1 Cor. 7:25–31). He saw how advantageous it would be to have single men and women undivided in their devotion to the Lord (verse 35). This is a theme that did not occur in the Old Testament. 'Paul is prescribing iron rations for hard times, which presaged the end of the present world-order.'[13] It would greatly encourage single women in their Christian service to be assured by their churches that they are God's messengers for such a time as this, and not in it *faute de mieux*. There are many signs that our world may be nearing the end of the era. We need to believe that God in his sovereignty has brought into the work of his kingdom many women without family attachments in order that they may fill gaps in the ranks which would otherwise remain unfilled.

As we look back to Genesis 2, its sublime teaching on the man/wife relationship establishes for all time the importance of its theme. Western Christendom has needed to be reminded that marriage is good, because the heresies that exalted celibacy have over the years exerted a pernicious influence that is slow to disappear. But it is not true to the biblical teaching as a whole to maintain that marriage is the only worthy calling for a woman and that anything else is second best.

> The narrative of Genesis 2 commits us to the integrity and freedom of the woman over against the man and of the man over against the woman, even as it commits us to their togetherness in an ineluctable relationship. This is the theology of the second creation narrative. . . . So far as Genesis 2 is concerned, sexual hierarchy must be read into the text; it is not required by the text.[14]

In the marriage relationship itself, as Jewett goes on to point out, the husband was the one who was to 'leave his father and his mother and cleave to his wife'. Contrary to

[13] F. F. Bruce, *Paul, Apostle of the Free Spirit* (Paternoster Press, 1977), p. 269.
[14] Paul K. Jewett, *op. cit.*, p. 126. Jewett's chapter headed 'The Relationship between Man and Woman' is full of important insights.

patriarchal practice, and indeed to Israelite custom through the centuries, Genesis 2:24 stands as witness to the divine order that the man should be the one to sever his ties with home to be joined to his wife. He is to go to her, not she to him.

To sum up, despite assertions to the effect that 'Genesis 2–3 sets out the divine order very clearly: man should obey God, woman obey man, and animals obey men and women', such interpretations must be questioned on biblical grounds.[15] 'We must obey God rather than men' (Acts 5:29) is applicable to women as well as men, and it would be extremely dangerous doctrine to assert otherwise. Moreover, even if Genesis 2 contained some law such as this interpretation suggests, the priority of the command of Jesus to go and make disciples of all the nations would override it.

Is there a 'creation ordinance'?: Genesis 1

This first chapter of Genesis, with majestic simplicity, establishes the perfection of God's creative work, accomplished by his word in exact accordance with his will. Here in the prime chapter on creation the Bible puts mankind in his place in God's universe and lays down major tenets for a doctrine of man. He is in God's image and likeness; he is given dominion within the created world; he is male and female. Because it is on our subject we shall concentrate on the last point, though all three are closely interrelated in the text, if not in the traditional exposition of the doctrine of man.

Western theology has not made much of the man/woman relationship, partly because of its heritage from sub-apostolic times, when the church was dogged by philosophies which exalted celibacy and urged the ascetic ideal, but partly also because the church's formative theologians, though they assumed that sexuality is a gift of God, saw little of importance in it for theology. Neither Augustine

[15] The quotation is from Gordon Wenham, 'The Ordination of Women: Why is it so divisive?' in *Churchman* 92, 4, 1978, p. 316; it is not easy to disagree with a friend whose opinions I value.

nor Thomas Aquinas thought in terms of the fellowship of man and woman having any bearing on the doctrine of the Trinity. Even Calvin broke no new ground here:

> ... He simply assumes what had not been questioned for centuries, that is, that the woman was given to the man as a helper in the one and only work in which he really needed her help, namely, the work of procreation.[16]

In general the duality of the sexes has been traditionally dealt with under the subject of marriage, with no attention to the implications of this duality. Thus the doctrine of man became entirely male-orientated and defined in male terms. But,

> *the primal form of humanity ... is the fellowship of man and woman.* How different is this from the approach of the philosophers and, to a less extent, of Christian theologians!... From a philosopher's standpoint this sexual dualism is a mere banality which (so it would seem) reminds us of Man's affinity with the animals rather than with God.[17]

That there has been for centuries in the church an erroneous masculinism was admitted by the late Michael Bruce in a definition of masculinism: 'the false idea that the only full members of the human race are male, and that women are second-class members of the human family'.[18] He recognized the challenge to theologians to deal more adequately with the fact that mankind was created male and female. We owe it largely to Karl Barth that theologians are becoming aware of the theological implications of this duality, and no doubt he is right in seeing this duality worked out mainly in marriage. Nevertheless the biblical doctrine of sexuality is wider than its doctrine of marriage, and needs to extend to the social

[16] Paul K. Jewett, *op. cit.*, p. 29.

[17] Paul K. Jewett, *op. cit.*, p. 36 (his italics).

[18] 'Heresy, Equality and the Rights of Women' in Michael Bruce and G. E. Duffield (eds.), *Why Not? Priesthood and the Ministry of Women* (Marcham Manor Press, 1972), pp. 42f.

and other general examples of co-operation between the sexes, so that there are theological guide-lines for men and women in Christian ministry as well as in other spheres.

The first chapter of Genesis provides the basis for such a theology. God created mankind in his own image, the two sexes together constituting 'man' (Gn. 1:27; *cf.* 5:2). If we would talk about the human race, then, we must have in mind men and women, for neither sex on its own is adequate. Dominion is given to both sexes without distinction (Gn. 1:28), no indication of a hierarchy being introduced. All mankind is here, without distinction of race or class. The one God has created all as one, and intends to deal with all on the same footing (*cf.* Gal. 3:28). Cassuto beautifully expresses the superb artistry of this chapter:

> The language . . . is tranquil, undisturbed by polemic or dispute; the controversial note is heard indirectly, as it were, through the deliberate, quiet utterances of Scripture, which set the opposing views at nought by silence or by subtle hint.[19]

Men and women in fellowship undertake the task of ordering the created world. No special division of labour is indicated, for a variety of possibilities is given to mankind to explore and develop. So rich are God's endowments that it is impossible to exhaust them in the lifetime of one individual man or woman, and millennia were to pass before the arts of pottery-making or writing were to develop. Amid today's unprecedented opportunities in music and the arts, science and technology, people have within their grasp the attainment of highly satisfying goals which at the same time give maximum benefit to the world. Economists and politicians give their minds to global strategy; doctors seek to eliminate the crippling diseases of the world; agriculturalists and biologists co-operate with other specialists to eliminate hunger. All this activity and much more comes within the scope of Genesis 1. No-one asks whether a man or a woman has authority

[19] U. Cassuto, *op. cit.*, p. 7.

in this or that sphere; competence for the task is all that is required.

Sad to say it is in the church, where discrimination is least in keeping, that women are debarred on the ground of their sex from full participation in ministry. In some evangelical circles the ground for this discrimination is summed up in a so-called 'creation ordinance', which should presumably be clear and unmistakable. But is there such an ordinance in Genesis 1 – 3? Is there some proto-historic canon here, fixed for ever in heaven, settling once and for all that women should not have authority or leadership? The question is not an academic one for women who hold appointments in theological and pastoral posts. It should not be forgotten that the Free Churches have ordained women for many years, that an increasing number of the Provinces of the Anglican Communion are doing so, and that all the denominations have long given their blessing to women founding churches and working in leadership training, preaching and teaching – provided the setting is another culture than their own. This procedure has been defended on the ground that the leader of the responsible sending body is male, and so the 'creation ordinance' is observed which requires the man to be the final authority!

As has already been pointed out, the opening chapter of the Bible does not suggest any hierarchical order of the sexes; the second lays stress on the man/wife relationship, but is its scope confined to marriage? The rabbis thought that when Genesis spoke of the woman being formed from the man, this implied that she was under man; but 'derivation does not entail subordination'.[20] Adam was made out of the dust of the earth, but no-one would argue that he was subordinate to it. Nor, as Jewett goes on to show, did temporal priority indicate superior worth or value.

If one were to infer anything from the fact that the woman was created after the man, it should be, in the light of the first creation narrative, that the woman is

[20] Paul K. Jewett, *op. cit.*, p. 126.

superior to the man. But if men do not find this conclusion palatable, let them ask themselves why women should stomach the rabbinic conclusion that the woman is inferior because created after the man.[21]

Moreover such a conclusion from creation proves too much. It would demand that throughout society in all ages God intended women to be under the authority of men. With a Queen on the English throne and several women Prime Ministers on the world scene, not to mention women in places of leadership in all walks of life, it would be ludicrous to urge that it is God's will that all should be demoted. One wonders whether those who put forward this viewpoint really take their own doctrine seriously. What they in fact demand is that *in the church* women should not be permitted any kind of authority over men which would upset the 'created order'. But why argue from a *creation* narrative and apply the argument only to the church? In my judgment we are intended to find in Genesis 2 basic principles for marriage; and in Genesis 1, God's 'Magna Carta' for men and women as they work together in God's world. 'Thus, when men and women work together in a professional capacity, they are equal partners, each responsible and directly accountable for their work.'[22]

Did the entrance of sin into the world so drastically alter the relationship between men and women that the Lord God pronounced a new decree to the effect that the man should have all authority and keep his wife in a subordinate role? We have seen that neither the standard commentaries nor the Hebrew syntax support such an interpretation. Indeed some who uphold the authority of husbands over wives object that this should be presented as a product of the curse, and find their line of reasoning rather in creation.[23] That there has been male domination

[21] *Ibid.*, p. 127.

[22] Joyce Baldwin, *You and the Ministry* (Church Pastoral Aid Society, 1979), p. 39.

[23] *E.g.* Thomas Howard, 'A Note from Antiquity on the Question of Women's Ordination', *Churchman* 92, 4, 1978, p. 328.

cannot be denied, but the glorious news of the gospel is that the second Adam came to the rescue and delivered our race from every kind of bondage.

Where then is the alleged 'divine ordinance' on the basis of which many churches throughout the world appoint only men to the ordained ministry and to other offices of responsibility? I have not heard it argued that men are holier, wiser or more capable than women. That would be difficult to prove. Instead it has become customary to find in the term 'creation ordinance' a master-stroke, which must in the interests of truth be challenged.

A matter of priorities

In conclusion, it seems to me that the argument about authority has been accorded an importance out of all proportion to Scripture's teaching on the subject, in much the same way that the fourth commandment assumed a disproportionate significance in the thinking (but not the practice) of Jesus' contemporaries (see Mt. 12:11). Our squabbles are reminiscent of the disciples' preoccupation with working out who was the greatest in the kingdom when Jesus was about to submit to crucifixion. The great commission of Jesus (Mt. 28:18–20) involves all believers and demands priority. In matters of organization and structure local churches are free to adopt whatever pattern is appropriate for their circumstances. No blueprint is provided in the New Testament. As for leadership, the New Testament is interested in moral and spiritual qualifications; it presupposes that human beings have the wit to apply appropriate criteria in the light of local needs and customs. Practice may vary, but fundamental attitudes are clear in Galatians 3:28.

Though there are examples in church history of occasions when the church has pioneered social change, it has more frequently been reactionary, as when arguing for a flat earth doctrine, or supporting the slave trade. The sad part is that scripture was quoted to support the reactionary attitudes. With hindsight it is possible to see that damage was done to the Christian cause, and we need to beware lest yet another example be added to the list of mistaken arguments from Scripture.

The role of women in the church

I. Howard Marshall

*Problems of interpretation · Women in the Gospels ·
The early church in the Acts · Some other New
Testament writers · The earlier epistles of Paul ·
The Pastoral Epistles · Conclusions*

Problems of interpretation

The role of women in the church in New Testament times
is one of those issues where most of the relevant evidence
is fairly straightforward, although some passages are as
difficult as any in the New Testament. The problem of
drawing conclusions for the practice of Christians today
is thus largely one of how to interpret the evidence. We
may list the problems as follows:

1. *There is the difficulty of determining what some
passages actually say, and of relating their teaching to
other passages which appear to present a different
outlook.* One might go so far as to say that the real
problem before us is how to relate together the apparently
contradictory statements in the New Testament, on the
assumption that there is a real underlying unity of
doctrine. We must be particularly careful not to attempt
superficial or artificial harmonizations.

2. *Some parts of the evidence are historical in that they
describe what happened in the early church, while other
parts are doctrinal in that they lay down principles or
precepts which ought to be followed.* Some scholars would
question whether we can deduce principles from the
historical examples in the New Testament, and would

insist that we must be guided primarily by the explicit principles. However, this does not mean that we set aside the historical examples as irrelevant; they show us how the principles were carried out and they may warn us against a false understanding of them.

3. *We have the problem of how to apply the New Testament teaching (given in specific circumstances and a particular cultural setting) to the church today in its different circumstances and cultural situation.* The guiding principle should be that when we encounter rules of conduct in the New Testament we ought to try to discover the underlying principles to which they give expression, and then ask how we can put those underlying principles into effect in our situation; in many cases the application may well be the same as in the first century, but in others the application may be somewhat different.

4. *The practice of the early Christians varied in different churches and at different times.* The names and functions of church leaders varied from place to place. Clearly the church today cannot take over the whole of New Testament practice. We must ask what basic principles are expressed in the different parts of the New Testament, and then devise a system appropriate to our situation which will be faithful to these principles, and the fact that different New Testament churches expressed them in different ways justifies the claim that there is a certain freedom and variety possible in the church today. For example, Baptist churches have a system of deacons (and, in some cases, elders) who fulfil the New Testament ideal of *diakonia* or service, but they are not necessarily to be faulted for not having officials called bishops, although these are equally scriptural, nor for having a local official called 'the secretary' who does not seem to have any specific New Testament equivalent. It should also be noted at this stage that the modern concept of 'the minister', in the sense of one person ordained by the laying on of hands to be (usually) the chief functionary in the local church and (usually) the one person authorized to celebrate the sacrament of the Lord's Supper, has no single counterpart in the New Testament.

Women in the Gospels

We shall now look at the relevant New Testament evidence, taking each appropriate historical or geographical section in turn. In the Gospels there is plenty of evidence that women responded to the message of Jesus and shared in the benefits of his ministry. Jesus could use women as examples of outstanding piety (Mk. 12:41–44; 14:3–9). At his crucifixion there were women present 'who, when he was in Galilee, followed him, and ministered to him; and also many other women who came up with him to Jerusalem' (Mk. 15:41); later some of them came to anoint his dead body, but were startled to find his tomb empty save for the presence of an angel who told them to go and tell his disciples that he was risen (Mk. 16:1–8). This brief summary, taken from a Gospel which, unlike Luke, does not go out of its way to stress the point, shows that the Evangelist presupposes a social setting in which women formed part of the group around Jesus. The following points, drawn from the Gospels generally, are important:

1. *The background to the ministry of Jesus was a Jewish society in which the character of married life and home life was not so very different from ours.* Religiously, however, the active part of women in the life of the temple and synagogue was becoming smaller. The priesthood had always been entirely male, although there still persisted isolated examples of women exercising prophetic gifts (Lk. 2:36). The synagogue services were conducted entirely by men, and during the first century women were increasingly segregated from men in the services. In general the Jewish rabbis regarded women as inferior to men. Against this background, Jesus' treatment of women as the religious equals of men so far as the privileges of the kingdom of God was concerned is highly significant.

2. *The twelve disciples who assisted Jesus in his mission were men, and the same may well have been true of the seventy(-two) who went out in pairs.* But here, whatever other considerations may have played a part, Jesus could well have been under the constraint of what was socially

acceptable, and it would have defeated his own purpose if he had chosen helpers whose sex would have hindered his work in a male-dominated society. We may compare the fact that in modern times missionary work among Indian women could not have been carried out by men, and so there developed the Zenana type of work carried out by women missionaries.

It is all the more significant, therefore, that the travelling entourage of Jesus included 'many' women who 'ministered' to Jesus and his companions and 'provided for them out of their means' (Lk. 8:3). This picture of a travelling group of both sexes – which incidentally does not seem to have been accused of any kind of sexual misconduct – is very different from what one might have expected in first-century Palestine. It suggests a trajectory pointing in a very different direction from that of orthodox Judaism. In other words, it would be wrong to take the evidence to mean that table-service and other tasks for the benefit of the male Christian workers were meant to be the limit of women's service; rather we should see here the first step towards a fuller sharing by women in the service of Christ, taken in a Jewish society that was far from congenial to such a new venture. This point is confirmed by the story of Mary and Martha in Luke 10:38–42; here Martha is discouraged from excessive preparations in the kitchen so that with Mary she may share in the teaching given by Jesus to his disciples.

3. *The first witnesses of the resurrection were women, despite the fact that Jewish law had little regard for the testimony of women, and it was these women who were charged to tell the story of the empty tomb to the apostles.* Here, and elsewhere, there is nothing incongruous about women acting as witnesses about Jesus to men (Jn. 4:28f., 39–42). It is not too much to say that already in the Gospels there is nothing in principle to forbid women from bearing witness about Jesus to men and fulfilling a ministry among his disciples. Any inhibiting factors arose from the social situation.

The early church in the Acts

The picture in Acts confirms this initial impression and takes us further. Women gathered with the men in the upper room in Jerusalem and devoted themselves to prayer (Acts 1:14), and we may be confident that they shared in the gift of the Spirit (Acts 1:15; 2:1). Indeed, the scripture quoted by Peter at Pentecost refers specifically to the participation of women in prophecy under the inspiration of the Spirit (Acts 2:17f.). The converts to the early church were both male and female (Acts 5:14). But the reconstituted group of the Twelve and the assistant group of Seven who were responsible for leadership were men, and again we may presume that the lack of place for women in the leadership of the church was dictated (at least in part) by the social and religious conventions of Judaism. In any case, Luke's picture of the church is lacking in detail, and there are many other points of which we remain ignorant.

Elsewhere in Acts we have the story of Tabitha (or Dorcas) at Joppa who was full of good works and acts of charity, especially to the widows in the church (always a needy group in ancient society when there were no pensions and social security payments), and conducted a home dressmaking service for their benefit (Acts 9:36–42). Here we have a good example of a woman doing a service that could not have been done equally well by men.

Among women converts in Acts there is Lydia. It seems likely that there was no synagogue in Philippi, probably because there were insufficient Jewish men (ten were required) to establish one. Lydia was the leading spirit in a small group of women who followed the Jewish faith and then gave hospitality to the missionaries. It would surely be unrealistic to suggest that when a small group of Christian women like this one was joined by the first male convert, they were not allowed to teach him and that he automatically took over the function of leadership.

At Corinth Paul met up with a Christian couple called Aquila and Priscilla. After the initial mention of the couple they are named as 'Priscilla and Aquila' (Acts 18:18, 26; *cf.* Rom. 16:3; 2 Tim. 4:19; contrast 1 Cor. 16:19). This reversed order shows that the wife was the more important and perhaps the more active as a Christian. They shared in Paul's Christian work as well as in their common trade of tentmaking, for later, when Paul left them in Ephesus, they befriended a preacher called Apollos in the synagogue and took him home with them to instruct him more adequately in the Christian faith.

Luke certainly intends us to understand that both Priscilla and Aquila were involved in this Christian instruction. It would be plainly contrary to the sense of the text to suppose that Priscilla merely served the coffee while the men did the speaking. Moreover, it would be totally anachronistic to draw a distinction between private and public, or between informal and formal instruction at this stage in the development of the church; we cannot employ such casuistry to play down the significant place of Priscilla.

Finally, Acts refers to the four unmarried daughters of Philip who were active as prophetesses at Caesarea (Acts 21:9). The comment is incidental and unemphatic, and it would be wrong to argue that because Luke records nothing of what they actually said they must have kept silent in the presence of a male prophet.

Although, then, for the most part men carried out the functions of evangelism and ministry in the churches described in Acts, there are cases of women exercising various forms of service. They took part in charitable care, but their activities were certainly not confined to this and included Christian instruction and prophecy.

Some other New Testament writers

Outside the Pauline epistles, there is admittedly little evidence for our purpose. Hebrews is not interested in the organization of the church, and contains only three references to church leaders (Heb. 13:7, 17, 24). These are expressed in masculine forms, but this does not necessarily exclude the possibility of some women as leaders along with the men, since the masculine was the correct grammatical form for a group of mixed sex. But there is nothing to show whether we should exploit this grammatical ambiguity.

James addresses his readers as 'brothers', and only at one point (Jas. 2:15) does it become clear that 'brothers' includes 'sisters'. He thinks in male terms, especially when he speaks about teachers and elders (Jas. 3:1; 5:14). This would not be surprising, if his milieu was largely Jewish-Christian.

1 Peter contains one passage about women being submissive to their husbands so that they may convert their non-Christian husbands by their silent witness (1 Pet. 3:1–5). It says nothing directly about what happened in a church meeting, although we might be tempted to assume that a society in which women had to keep silent about their faith at home was unlikely to encourage them to take a leading part in the life of the church. However, it must be emphasized that the restriction on verbal witness to their husbands was probably culturally based; the Christian cause would not be helped by women who took unheard-of liberties in trying to convert husbands who expected them to be submissive – and surely nobody would want to claim today that a wife who became converted should not speak to her husband about her faith. Indeed, one might well argue that it was precisely *because* Christian women had a new-found freedom to speak in church meetings, that Peter had to warn them that carrying over their freedom of speech into their non-Christian home situation might be counter-productive.

The other epistles contain nothing relevant for us. The 'elect lady' in 2 John (1, 13) is probably a personification of the church and not a real person (the same interpretation is generally taken of 1 Pet. 5:13). 3 John mentions travelling missionaries who are simply called 'the brothers'.

In Revelation (2:20–23) there is a woman called Jezebel who gave herself out to be a prophetess and led the church astray. This shows that the activity of women in prophecy was accepted; the author's attack on her – seen pointedly in the nickname 'Jezebel' – was directed against her false teaching and not against her sex.

I. Howard Marshall

The earlier epistles of Paul

Paul's earliest epistles, to Galatia and Thessalonica, address the congregations as 'brothers', a term that must have included women. The church at Corinth obviously included women among its members. Romans 16:1f. conveys a commendation of Phoebe who is described as a 'deacon' of the church at Cenchreae, which was one of the two seaports of Corinth; she had been of help to many people, including Paul himself. She can be assumed to have carried the letter to Rome, and from her name she was a Gentile. There is general agreement that the term *diakonos* describes her specific office in the church as a deacon (*cf.* Phil. 1:1; 1 Tim. 3:8–13). It is commonly assumed that the tasks of deacons were related to practical service for the needy (Rom. 12:7; 1 Pet. 3:11; note, however, that the Seven in Acts 6 are *not* called deacons, that their 'service' of tables stands alongside 'service' of the Word (Acts 6:2, 4), and that two of the Seven distinguished themselves as evangelists); deacons need not necessarily have been confined to this one duty.

The same chapter contains a list of people in Rome to whom Paul sends greetings. They include Prisca (an abbreviated form of Priscilla) and Aquila, described as Paul's fellow workers in Christ Jesus (Rom. 16:3). This phrase is of crucial importance. It undoubtedly means that they were Paul's full colleagues in missionary service, and the way in which Paul, like Luke, places Prisca first confirms that she was an active missionary. Nothing indicates that her work was purely among women. Other missionary couples are mentioned in 1 Corinthians 9:5, although it is arguable that there the wives are companions for their husbands rather than colleagues in service. The list in Romans continues with 'Mary, who has worked hard among you', Tryphaena, Tryphosa and Persis, who are all workers in the Lord, and other women who are simply members of the church. 'Work' is 'missionary work', and the same words are used of male missionaries as well as female (Rom. 16:6, 12; *cf.* 1 Cor. 15:10, 58; 2 Cor. 10:15). Of particular interest is a reference to Junia (the RSV identifies this person as a male, 'Junias', but it is highly probable that the name is that of a woman), who is a person 'of note among the apostles', *i.e.* an apostle. This means that Junia was an apostle; either one of the group, larger than the Twelve, who saw the risen Lord and was called to missionary service (1 Cor. 15:7), or one of the group sent out by the churches on missionary service (2 Cor. 8:23; Phil. 2:25).

At Philippi we have Euodia and Syntyche, who 'have laboured side by side with me in the gospel together with Clement and the rest of my fellow workers' (Phil. 4:2f.). This indicates some sort of team-effort and does not hint at separate work by the women. There was a house church at Laodicea which met in the house of Nympha (Col. 4:15; the name is most probably a feminine form).

These references show that women played a considerable part in the missionary work of Paul. He describes them as his helpers and colleagues in mission work, in exactly the same way as he describes men. Since the organization of the church was still fairly informal, the implication is that Paul saw them as, in principle, performing the same kind of tasks as he himself was doing. There is nothing to suggest that the women engaged in missionary work confined their activities either to practical help or to evangelization among their own sex. We could assume this only if the social and cultural background was such that women were naturally confined to such functions. But this was not the case in the Hellenistic world which was the sphere of Christian mission, and we have the explicit evidence that Priscilla instructed Apollos.

We must now ask whether Paul's explicit statements of principle fit in with the principles already implicit in this historical survey. It should be clear that if Paul accepted women as his fellow workers, he is unlikely to have denied them this possibility in his teaching.

In Galatians 3:28 we have an early statement by Paul to the effect that a person's religious and racial background makes no difference to his acceptability to God if he believes in Jesus. In Christ Jesus we are all sons of God, whether we are Jews or Greeks. This statement is enough to establish Paul's immediate point, but he proceeds to enlarge it, saying that it is also true, whether we are slaves or free, male or female: 'for you are all one in Christ Jesus'. The expansion of thought is not a piece of rhetoric. It must deal with what were real issues in the church, since Paul repeats it elsewhere (1 Cor. 12:13; Col. 3:11). A person was no less the object of divine grace and the divine call if he was a slave. Similarly, both men and women were equally objects of God's grace. Hence in the new situation brought about by the death and resurrection of Jesus all Christians are 'one', in the sense that they belong together in the one family of God as brothers and sisters; there should be no hatred or rivalry between them, and nobody should regard himself as superior to anybody else or place his own interests before theirs. Thus Paul denies that in the eyes of God – and therefore in the eyes of his people – Jews are 'better' than Gentiles, or free men than slaves, or men than women. Obviously this cannot mean that the differences of race, social position and sex are obliterated, but it does mean that they do not matter in fixing a person's status and value.

In practice this meant that Jews and Gentiles must consider one another as brothers and sisters, and similarly with free men and slaves (*cf.* Phm. 16). But this new relationship in the church was bound to affect their social relationships. A master could no longer treat his slaves as chattels on Monday if he was on terms of brotherhood with them on Sunday; although it took a long time for the church to realize it, it implied that the whole concept of slavery was unchristian, even if the New Testament itself does not say so explicitly. Similarly, it implied that the racial barriers which, for example, forbade Jews to eat with Gentiles no longer existed, so that the concept of race became irrelevant in social relationships. In this context it is interesting that again the church took some time to achieve complete freedom on this issue. In Acts 15:28f. the Gentile Christians were required to abstain from blood and non-kosher meat in order not to alienate Jewish Christians; we never hear explicitly that this requirement was countermanded, but in practice it ceased to be observed, and nobody would suggest that it is still authoritative today despite the lack of explicit withdrawal of the rule.

But what of the male/female relationship? It certainly meant an end to the attitude in which a man could treat his wife as a lesser being and impose his will upon her. In 1 Corinthians 7, a chapter which has often been thought falsely to betray a low view of marriage, Paul insists that husband and wife have equal rights in the most intimate of their relationships; if the husband 'rules' over his wife's body, it is equally true that she 'rules' (a strong word) over his. Decisions about physical relationships must be made in the light of these complementary principles. If the wife is told to be subject to her husband (an instruction given in a situation where the characteristic tendency of woman as a sinner is to be self-willed), the husband is told to love his wife (an instruction given in a situation where the characteristic tendency of man as a sinner is to be domineering). If both partners fulfil these commands, the result will be a relationship of equality. When Paul and Peter counsel wives to be subject to their husbands, they have very much in mind the situation of a Christian wife married to a non-Christian husband who expected obedience from her; she would be more likely to convert him to the faith by submission than by irritating him through practising 'women's lib.'. In general, Paul and Peter expect their readers to fulfil their side of the relationship even when the other partner fails to do so (the slave must still obey his master, even if the master fails to treat the slave fairly).

The teaching in 1 Corinthians 11:2–16 must be seen in the light of this basic principle. Here it is assumed that women pray and prophesy in a church meeting, and Paul's concern is with how this should be done, not with the question whether it should be done. We need, however, to look briefly at what Paul says about the women's use of a veil or a particular hair-style.[1]

Firstly, although Paul insists on the 'headship' of the

[1] See the discussions by C. Brown, *The New International Dictionary of New Testament Theology*, II, pp. 159–162; J. B. Hurley, *Man and Woman in Biblical Perspective*, pp. 162–194.

husband over the wife, and insists that woman is the glory of man, this is no obstacle to a woman praying or prophesying. The priority of husband over wife is safe-guarded by her covering her head. Secondly, when Paul says that the woman should have 'authority' on her head (1 Cor. 11:10, RSV mg., rendering the Greek correctly), her head-covering is the symbol of her authority, and means that she does have authority to take part in the church meeting. Thirdly, Paul argues that if it is natural for a woman to have long hair (in contrast to the shorter hair of men) to cover her, it is also appropriate for her to cover herself with a veil. (Scholars debate, however, whether Paul is commending a particular hair-style (so J. B. Hurley) or the use of a veil.) Fourthly, Paul's instructions are given in the context of a church composed of both Jews and Gentiles. The shaven head was a Jewish punishment for adultery. It may well be that behind Paul's instructions lies a situation in which the women were taking part in the church meeting with a hair-style which shocked the more conservative Jewish Christians. Paul's requirement that they be dressed appropriately may be a compromise, to avoid offending the Jews (who would have regarded a woman taking any part in the meeting as a sufficiently shocking thing); but he endeavours to base it on stronger grounds of principle.

When we attempt to apply this passage to contemporary society, two things must be said. First, the social and cultural situation is different. Few people regard a woman who takes part in a meeting as doing something strange or as dishonouring her husband. A particular ancient hair-style or a veil (still less a hat) simply does not have what-ever significance it had in Paul's time, so that adoption of this practice does not achieve whatever purpose Paul had in mind. A literal obedience to Paul's command does not fulfil the command. But, second, the underlying principles which Paul was trying to maintain are still to be main-tained. The church has still to bear witness to the fact that 'the head of a woman is her husband' (and that husbands must love their wives), and therefore something may need to be said about the manner in which women take part in a service. It was all too easy for women in the Corinthian church to behave excessively in their enthusiasm for their new-found emancipation in Christ; the influence of extreme Women's Lib. movements today may also lead to excesses and unchristian behaviour.

Prayer and prophecy were forms of ministry in the church. The former is not regarded as a special charisma, although praying in tongues was so regarded (1 Cor. 14:14–19). But prophecy was a gift of the Spirit, who gives his gifts to each individual as he wills. It is likely that Paul uses prophecy in a fairly wide sense to cover various kinds of inspired utterance (just as Luke does), although in 1 Corinthians 12 and 14 various types of inspired utterance are distinguished. But in any case there does not seem to be any reason why women, who were allowed to prophesy, should not also have 'a hymn, a lesson, a revelation, a tongue or an interpretation' (1 Cor. 14:26). If we bear in mind the apparent fluidity in the terminology, it would seem to follow that women could take part in any of the verbal aspects of the church meeting. In particular, if a woman could 'prophesy' in Corinth, it is difficult to see why she may not 'preach' in Aberdeen.

But what about the specific instruction which follows Paul's advice about the church meeting: 'As in all the churches of the saints, the women should keep silence in the churches' (1 Cor. 14:34f.)? It has been argued that Paul here withdraws the permission given to the women to pray and prophesy in 1 Corinthians 11. But, quite apart from the fact that we believe that the teaching of Scripture should form a harmonious whole, it is wholly out of the question that Paul should in effect contradict what he had just said three chapters earlier. Various other solutions to the difficulty have been suggested.

1. *Verses 34 and 35 are transferred in some manuscripts to a position after verse 40.* When this sort of thing happens, it is sometimes a sign that the movable verses did not originally belong to the text. If so, the verses would not be a part of Scripture but a comment by a later scribe. However, the textual evidence for omission is not strong

here, and there is nothing in the language and style of the verses to show that they are not by Paul. This solution is unlikely.

2. *Paul may have been distinguishing between prayer and prophecy (which are permitted) and teaching (which is not permitted).* But it is hard to see how prophecy and teaching would be distinguished. Certainly inspired prophecy must have been as authoritative as teaching.

3. *Some of the disorder which Paul was attempting to curb at Corinth may well have arisen from the activities of the women, and Paul felt it right to command them to be silent,* just as he could command that an individual male prophet must be silent in certain circumstances. He may have been concerned about women chattering or otherwise disturbing the church meeting. In particular, verse 35 suggests that they may have been asking questions in church, and generally acting in a way which may have brought feelings of shame and embarrassment to their husbands. In other words, Paul was dealing with a specific situation where a particular form of activity appeared shameful to a congregation who believed in the subordination of the wife to her husband.

4. *The restriction may apply only to speaking in tongues or to the judging of prophets (1 Cor. 14:29).* The latter could have involved adopting a position that seemed inconsistent with a woman's position.

It is difficult to adjudicate between possibilities 3 and 4. J. B. Hurley has argued well in favour of view 4, in which case Paul's command is concerned with a practice that is only marginally present in the modern church situation, if at all. It is probable that view 3 also expresses correctly something of the background to Paul's command. What is important is that Paul bases his advice on principles. Women are to be subject to their own husbands in accordance with the teaching of the law (Gn. 3:16 is generally reckoned to be the passage Paul had in mind), and it is 'shameful' for a woman to speak in church. It is not obvious, however, that in contemporary society and the contemporary church a woman who took part in a service would be regarded as showing insubordination to her husband or that it would seem shameful – although again we must bear in mind that a woman (or a man) may minister out of sinful, self-centred and arrogant motives. Obedience, then, to Paul's principles does not tie us to the letter of his precept; there is no reason why a woman may not participate in a church service from pure and lofty motives, and exercise whatever spiritual gifts the Spirit may bestow on her.

The Pastoral Epistles

The final passage which must be considered is 1 Timothy 2:8–15. Here we must bear in mind that the Pastoral Epistles envisage a situation in which some people were forbidding marriage (probably for ascetic reasons, 1 Tim. 4:3), some of the younger widows were becoming idlers, gossips and busybodies (1 Tim. 5:13), and there were some women who were 'weak . . . burdened with sins and swayed by various impulses, who will listen to anybody and can never arrive at a knowledge of the truth' (2 Tim. 3:6f.). We may well postulate a situation in which some women had been making a nuisance of themselves in the church by teaching, and others were easily yielding to false teaching. We are also at a stage when in the churches in question (Ephesus and Crete) there was a tendency to more formal organization; there was a roll or list of widows who received some kind of financial assistance and were expected to be pious and given to good works (1 Tim. 5:3–16; *cf.* Tit. 2:3f.). The churches were under the pastoral care of men such as Timothy and Titus who had supervisory roles like that of Paul himself and are the nearest thing in the New Testament to the modern 'super-intendent' or 'bishop'. In the local churches there were elders/bishops (the terms appear to be synonymous) and deacons – leaders who, it is interesting to note, are not mentioned in 1 Corinthians 12:28.

In every place ('where Christians gather' is implied) it should be the men who pray (here the word in its context is restricted to the male sex), doubtless in an audible manner. The next verse (1 Tim. 2:9) begins with an 'also', and it is not certain whether the clause is a continuation of the construction in verse 8 and describes how women should attire themselves at prayer, or whether it simply describes how they should dress and implies that they are not envisaged as praying. The former possibility seems more likely, and is in accord with the practice reflected elsewhere in the New Testament. The main point, however, is that in church meetings (and probably at other times) the women should deport themselves modestly and adorn themselves with good deeds rather than with an outward show of dress and jewellery. The references to modesty and good sense suggest that the concern is that the women should not dress in such a way as to divert the men from prayer by sexual enticement or worldly show. Verses 11 and 12 go on to state that a woman must learn in submissiveness, and not teach and lord it over the man. Here teaching is regarded as the expression of an attitude of superiority to the man, and it is essentially this attitude of superiority which is opposed. The subordinate place of woman is related to the fact that Eve was created subsequently to Adam, and in this temporal priority of Adam there is seen the expression of some kind of ontological priority. Eve too was the first to sin, through being deceived by the serpent. It is even said that she was deceived and not Adam, and if one were to reply that Adam nevertheless fell into sin through Eve's temptation, he would possibly have contended that the fact that Eve deceived Adam merely demonstrates that a deceived woman is a source of danger to her husband. The woman will be saved in her role of bearing children and must show Christian virtues.

In attempting to understand and apply the passage we may observe, on the one hand, that the stress on the place of women in raising and bringing up their families (perhaps originally directed against an ascetic revulsion from sexual intercourse and childbearing) needs to be repeated in a society where the lack of maternal care (and easy divorce) is detrimental to the welfare of children. The warnings against sexual seductiveness and worship at the shrine of the goddess Fashion may also not be out of place. On the other hand, the insistence on the silence of women, which appears to run contrary to practice earlier in the church, may be partly due to an unfortunate experience in an unusual and difficult situation. At the very least, women are to be allowed to learn, which is more than a Jewish teacher would have permitted! The insistence in the passage on the prior place of the man, as indicated in the creation story, cannot be ignored; but it is surely the case that in the modern situation, where a woman's teaching does not call this relationship in question, it should be permissible for her to teach.

The liability of women to be deceived and hence to give erroneous instruction is also stressed. But we must ask whether it is the case that women are more liable to be deceived than men. If men who teach must at all times beware lest they communicate error, but must nevertheless practise this ministry, it would seem equally proper that women also, despite their being in the same danger, should exercise a ministry of teaching. Nor is there any evidence that women may safely teach other women without falling into error, but must not teach men. Finally, even if women do bear children, not all women *can* do so, and the task does not exclude other forms of activity; it cannot be meant that attention to rearing a family is an adequate substitute for ministry in the church.

Much has been made of the fact that while 1 Timothy 3 allows for the appointment of female deacons (verse 11), there is no mention of any female elders. It is then assumed that the elders were the teachers and that women were excluded from this role. But there are several uncertainties about this argument. Firstly, it is not certain that verse 11 refers to female deacons; it may refer to the wives of deacons. Secondly, 1 Timothy 5:17 suggests that not all elders were active in preaching and teaching. Thirdly, the epistle assumes that men will be appointed as elders and deacons, and it does not explicitly forbid the appointment of women to either function. Fourthly, the precise duties of church leaders and the relative allocation of them between elders and deacons remain vague. Fifthly, the modern 'minister' and the ancient 'elder' cannot be simply

identified with one another. What is true, then, is that in
1 Timothy the elders and deacons are men (with possibly
some women deacons); married women are apparently
occupied with the care of their family; younger widows
are encouraged to remarry; and older widows (and
presumably older single women) are expected to do good
deeds, pray and set an example of godliness. Nothing
suggests that this is an inviolable pattern for all time, and,
as we have seen, it was not the universal pattern in the
early church.

Conclusions

We have seen that women were to be found as fellow
missionaries with Paul, doing Christian work in local
churches, praying, prophesying and giving instruction, and
also carrying out duties for which they were better suited
than men, such as caring for the sick and needy and
showing hospitality. In the light of this historical sketch,
Paul's recognition that women prayed and prophesied in
the church at Corinth makes good sense. Paul, however,
was insistent that women who took part in church meetings should avoid doing anything which might seem to go
against the principle of subordination to their husbands
which he took from the Old Testament; equality in Christ
did not mean lording it over their menfolk. However, in
1 Timothy we found what is often seen as a total ban on
women taking part in ministry, other than in private
prayer and good works. The problem is how we reconcile
these differing pictures and apply the biblical teaching to
the church today.

1. At the risk of repetition we again emphasize that *the
New Testament picture is a mixed one*, of women taking
part in church meetings and of women being commanded
to be silent.

2. We have seen the principles to which the New Testament writers appeal when they command women to be
silent, but we have also seen that *the particular way in
which these commands were framed may reflect specific
first-century circumstances*. In Corinth it is likely that

women were abusing their new-found freedom in Christ in a way that was bringing the church into disrepute, especially among men of a Jewish background. In the situation envisaged in 1 Timothy the women were particularly liable to be attracted by false teaching; some of them were refusing marriage and the rearing of children. In both situations women may have been using their opportunities for teaching to vaunt themselves over the men. If these dangers had not needed to be curbed, the practical implications of the basic principles might have been different.

3. *Paul appeals to principles when discussing the place of women.* On the one hand, there is no inferiority of females to males in the church. Just as Gentiles and slaves could share in the work of the gospel and ministry alongside Jews and free men, so women did so alongside men. On the other hand, the distinction between male and female cannot be imagined away; biology is a fact of creation. The equality of men and women does not obliterate the distinction between the sexes. For Paul the husband is the 'head' of his wife. She is to obey him and he is to love her. Equality in Christ does not mean that she is now to lord it over him or that he need not honour her as (in general) the physically weaker person (1 Pet. 3:7). Instead, the differences between the sexes must be seen in the light of the new creation in which love is the supreme principle. Where, then, a women uses her position in the church to vaunt herself over her husband or other men, she is misusing it and is guilty of pride. But equally of course the man must not use his position in an arrogant or loveless manner.

In the ancient world, especially in the situation where women were being emancipated from their inferior status in Judaism, it may have been easy for women to feel superior to men if they took part in a church meeting, and to assert themselves deliberately over the men; and it would have been easy for the men to feel humiliated by the new attitude of the women. Similar problems arose with regard to Jew/Gentile relationships. But in the modern Western situation where the emancipation of women is a fact (largely thanks to Christian influence), it is surely the case that these feelings have largely disappeared. We are accustomed to men and women teaching and leading one another without feeling that the dignity of either sex is being assailed. Nor is it the case that advocates of the silence of women in church reject the possibility of Christian women occupying roles in the secular community in which they may teach and lead mixed groups of men and women. In this situation, where the principles of creation and redemption are not infringed by women taking part in ministry, we may well conclude that it is right and proper for them to do so.

4. *It is arguable that, just as the church has moved beyond the New Testament toleration of slavery to a recognition that Christian principles forbid slavery, so too can we with a good conscience accept a larger place for women in the ministry of the church than was possible in first-century society.* The trajectory which apparently leads through the Pastoral Epistles to the rigid clamping down on the place of women in the post-apostolic church and on into many modern churches is a false one; rather, recognizing that the Pastoral Epistles were concerned to deal with a real abuse in their time, we may argue that the true line of advance should be traced from Jesus through the earlier epistles of Paul and onwards in the direction of the equality of God's people in his church. There were good social and cultural reasons why the early church 'hastened slowly' in giving women a vital role in the church and its ministry, thus restraining potentially dangerous developments at the time. In the world of today, we can move more readily to a full appreciation of the part that women can play in the church.

5. *The preaching of the word in the New Testament took various forms and was undertaken by a variety of people in any local church (and nothing is said to indicate who would preside at the Lord's Supper).* If, however, women could and did take part in the less formal ministries that then existed, there is no reason why they should not so function today. If the early church gave the opportunities it did to Priscilla and Junia who ranked high among Paul's colleagues, have we any right to close such

opportunities to women today, or to restrict the possibility of them to the increasingly anachronistic area known as 'the mission field overseas'?

Response to Joyce Baldwin and Howard Marshall

Daphne Key

At the heart of Joyce Baldwin's article is her interpretation of Genesis 1 – 3. She asserts that Genesis 1 is the basis of an equality between men and women which should result in equal opportunities in every sphere of life. She sees Genesis 2 as providing principles which apply only to marriage. Only in Genesis 3 does she detect grounds for male/female role differences, arguing that these resulted from the fall. This view does not take into account the significance of man's prior creation, nor of his naming of the woman, which Jim Hurley has expounded in this book. A scholar whom she herself quotes, Delitzsch, says on Genesis 3:

> The sub-ordination of woman to man was intended from the beginning but now that the harmony of their mutual wills in God is destroyed this subordination becomes subjection.

When we look at how the Bible itself uses Genesis 1 – 3 (*i.e.* in 1 Cor. 11:11 and 1 Tim. 2:8f.) we may deduce more from these chapters than Joyce Baldwin might allow, especially from Genesis 2. I would agree that Genesis 1 says nothing about division of labour between the sexes, but Genesis 2 does lay down principles for such a division. Genesis 3, rather than being the basis of an argument for differences of role between men and women in the church, explains the sorry state of relationships between men and women in this fallen world. And it is from the curse of Genesis 3 that Christians are being saved, experiencing something of the ideal (illustrated in Genesis 1 and 2) of the equality before God of both men and women and yet of their God-given differences.

Howard Marshall's article furnishes us with helpful illustrations of the avenues of service open to women in the church, and I would beg to differ with him on only two points. The first is that in his interpretation of 1 Corinthians 14, he equates prophecy in New Testament times with modern preaching. This leads him to the conclusion that if women could 'prophesy in Corinth' they may now 'preach in Aberdeen'! But I would not regard the terms as synonymous, and would therefore disagree with his conclusion (see my footnote on p. 144 of my article).

Secondly I would disagree with the conclusions he draws from 1 Timothy 2. Although he states that Paul's 'insistence on the prior place of man as indicated in creation cannot be ignored', he is guilty of doing precisely that in allowing that women may take part in the church's regular authoritative ministry of the word of God. I would argue, with Paul, that the creation order remains valid and that this is one biblical application of this creation principle. If this were not so, why would Paul use the argument from creation?

In conclusion I would urge both men and women to participate fully in the life of the Christian community but to do it in such a way as to demonstrate, not only their oneness in Christ, but also their complementary God-given roles.

Response to Howard Marshall and Joyce Baldwin

James B. Hurley

Howard Marshall rightly asks us to distinguish between the abiding principles of the New Testament and the culture which helped shape their application. His central thesis is that the early Pauline churches were informally organized with women freely participating in many kinds of 'ministry' (*diakonia*, service). He tells us that many of these informal 'ministries' became tasks restricted to men or to elders in the more rigidly structured later Pauline churches of Timothy and Titus. Howard suggests that the restricting of teaching and authority in the later Pauline churches was situationally, not theologically, demanded; and that modern reservation of certain functions to 'clergy' is a mistake. We should choose the early rather than the later Pauline model and allow women to serve in every area of church life.

I concur that the church has often defined the elder/bishop's role in a way that bans non-elders (laity) from legitimate service (ministry) in the church. I disagree with Howard concerning: 1. the unstructured informality of the early church; 2. the relation between the 'ministries' of women and the office of elders; and 3. the situational relativization of Paul's theologically based instructions in 1 Timothy 2.

1. *Organizational structures in the early church.* I see

no reason to question the appointment of authoritative (male) elders as Paul's standard practice in his early churches. Luke describes Paul as addressing the elders of his Ephesian congregation concerning their role as overseers (*episkopoi*) guarding God's flock (Acts 20:18, 28). Philippians is addressed to overseers and deacons (Phil. 1:1).

2. *Women's ministries and the eldership.* The fact that women are found in ministry (service, *diakonia*) in the early church does not mean they were elders. It is only Howard's developmental hypothesis which leads to this conclusion. Then, as now, non-elders did many things which elders also do. Further, I do not understand 1 Timothy 2 to prohibit women from *all* ministry (as Howard argues). The discussion of widows and the possibility of women deacons in chapter 3 refutes this.

3. *Situational relativization of 1 Timothy 2.* In my contribution I have explained why I do not believe we can dismiss Paul's theological argument in 1 Timothy 2 as culturally specific and not applicable today.

Joyce Baldwin's paper is an eloquent plea for recognition of the dignity and worth of women. With this I joyfully concur. Her development of the view that, possessing dignity and worth, women should be ministers is less convincing. My contribution addresses many of the points which she makes. I will not repeat them all here but note only some points about her paper which I think important.

1. *The rejection of and appeal to the Old Testament.* Joyce argues that any Old Testament law regarding women should be reviewed in the light of Christ. Arguments based on Old Testament priestly precedent or even Jesus' practice 'lack cogency because they are arguments from the old order ... [which] has passed away'. As presented, this sort of position undercuts *all* Old Testament authority in every area. Joyce clearly does not intend to argue this, for she uses the bulk of her space to show that what the Old Testament *really* teaches ought to be embraced. Her effort to identify the prohibition of women

as elders with Saturday sabbath-keeping points up a major problem relating the Testaments. Her solution calls in question the legitimacy of Christians using the Old Testament in any manner.

2. *Apparent rejection of (what I take to be) Pauline teaching.* Joyce follows Paul Jewett in rejecting as 'rabbinic' the idea that 'derivation entails subordination'. She does not directly impute this view to Paul. Jewett, whom she favourably cites, does so expressly (p. 119), insisting that this idea cannot be harmonized with Paul's own 'greater Christian vision' (pp. 112–113). I believe Jewett is right that Paul argues that the headship of the husband is related to the fact that 'the man is not out of the woman but the woman out of the man' (1 Cor. 11:9). Jewett is wrong in inferring contradiction, or that subordination implies inferiority. On my reading, at least, Joyce seems to reject as 'rabbinic' a view which even Jewett agrees is advanced by Paul the apostle. I believe this is a problem for her view.

3. *Valuable rejection of selected views.* Joyce rightly dismisses a number of views traditionally held, especially those which impute inferiority to women or imply no woman may ever teach anywhere.

4. *There are alternatives.* I am not convinced by Joyce's handling of Genesis 1 – 3. I suspect she is not happy with mine. I have tried to address views such as hers in my text.

5. *Genesis 2:24: Leaving the husband's home.* The husband's leaving his father and mother to go to his wife is not necessarily contrary to patriarchal practice. It does not necessarily mean leaving the camp of his father. It does mean leaving the authority of his father's home to establish a new house with his wife. Women always left their home at marriage. The text is telling us about the establishment of a new social unit in the establishing of a new marriage.

Where do we go from here?

Shirley Lees

Clearly Christians who take the authority of Scripture seriously do differ on what the Bible actually says and means on the subject of women. Some of the differences seem quite wide. In drawing the threads together, we need to remind ourselves afresh of the fact that Scripture never contradicts itself. If we appear to make it do so, then it is our finite minds and understanding which are at fault. We are creatures of our culture (which in many cases is one of long-standing male superiority). We have our denominational backgrounds and emphases of interpretation. We are subject to preconceived understanding of certain words, the connotations of which are affected by our cultural backgrounds. But even without prejudice, those who have made lifelong studies of Hebrew and Greek can still have differences of opinion as to the meaning of words. Once again, therefore, we must express our gratitude to our contributors to this symposium for their willingness to expose themselves to criticism, both from one another and from you, the readers.

As we look at the contributions to the first section of the debate, we find that there is no disagreement over the statements in Genesis that we all, male and female, are created in God's image and that woman was created as a 'helper' for man. The only thing that God saw in his initial creation that was 'not good' was that man was alone. All are agreed, too, that with the fall came male dominance and female subjection, but whether that was a statement of the result of the fall or God's judgment on sin is open to question. There is also a fundamental disagreement on what it means to be a 'helper', and whether there was a hierarchical structure or partnership of equals before the fall.

Valerie Griffiths illustrates the way in which woman completes the wholeness of mankind and that the command to subdue the earth was given to mankind, male and female. She stresses that a wife can remain as a helper 'fit for' her husband only when she is fulfilled in herself and stimulated as a thinking, rational person. Elizabeth Catherwood, on the other hand, sees such fulfilment in having, as her primary role, that of support for her husband and family at every level – physically, emotionally, mentally and spiritually. She points out that the ideal woman of Proverbs 31 runs her household and family so efficiently in her role of helper that her husband is free 'to take his place as a leader in the outside world'. Valerie Griffiths also looks at Proverbs 31 and suggests that here was 'a business woman who ran a home industry and staff so efficiently that her husband could trust her and leave her to act, even in the buying of property'. It is an interesting difference of emphasis and perhaps the difference mainly demonstrates the fact that the Ideal Woman really was the ideal 'helper'. She had a perfect balance between her care and support of her husband and her capacity to use her abilities to the full in a variety of ways.

Whatever 'helper' means, it does not mean that the woman is in any way inferior to the man. Any idea of inferiority must come from a misunderstanding of Scripture, probably due to the male-dominated culture of previous generations. This idea of inferiority is not however just a thing of the past. Although all our present contributors are agreed that helper does not mean inferior, Michael Griffiths points out that there is still 'a patronizing superior attitude in some Christian men towards women'. This is bolstered by an interpretation of Genesis which teaches a hierarchy 'which must imply superiority of one party over the other'. Nevertheless he agrees with David Field that the Bible teaches headship, and they both clearly outline the areas of meaning covered by the word. David Field, with his 'delicately tuned balance', comes to the conclusion that the idea of authority is there – loving, giving *and* authority – but sees no room whatever for this implying superiority. Michael Griffiths on the other hand sees it as meaning loving and giving *rather than* authority, especially as the word authority is 'hardly ever used in the context of husband-wife relations'.

Michael Griffiths helpfully shows us the degrees of meaning of submission and reminds us that nowhere in Scripture is the husband told to subject his wife to himself. Any submission is voluntary, a view which Elizabeth Catherwood whole-heartedly endorses. She exhorts women to rejoice in this opportunity to show Christian humility. It is to be 'as to the Lord' and she reminds us that 'God's laws for society are never harsh or constricting, but are so planned that those who live by them are happier and more secure than those who spend their time fighting for dominance or self-expression'.

That we, as Christians, should submit to one another is not a point of difference. Paul tells us that we should 'in humility consider others better than yourselves' and that our 'attitude should be the same as that of Christ' (Phil. 2:3, 5). The self-assertive wife who wants her 'rights' and to 'do her own thing' does not seem to be giving herself with the self-giving humility that is enjoined on *all* believers. Equally the self-assertive husband who keeps his wife 'in her place' and wants to 'do his own thing' does not seem to be living out the injunction to 'love as Christ loved the church and gave himself for it'. To repeat the quotation which Valerie Griffiths gives us from Marlene Cohen: 'Any self assertion (male or female) that seeks its own right at the expense of others, cannot be condoned.' Whether partnership of equals or hierarchy of headship and submission, Christian marriage is giving and receiving, not giving and taking.

As we try to sort out our own thinking, it has been

helpful to look at what the headship of Christ means. We see in him complete submission to the Father while at the same time he is completely equal with the Father. The Father has submitted all things to him and he has authority over all creation and the church. He is pre-eminent. But as we look at his authority, any idea of domineering is abolished. Both Michael Griffiths and David Field point out that Jesus contrasted the way 'the kings of the Gentiles lord it over' their subjects with the way he wants his followers to act: 'The one who rules should be the one who serves.' And as David Field shows us, 'Jesus did not step down from his position of authority when he washed the disciples' feet.' 'You call me Lord . . . and *rightly so*, for that is what I am.' But as he said it, he was doing the job of a slave.

As in all things, Scripture has a perfect balance. Submission is not subjugation, as Elizabeth Catherwood shows us. Pointing out that nowhere in Scripture are women 'reduced to brainless ciphers', she demonstrates the strength of character, wisdom and determination to do God's will of many of the women of the Bible. She also suggests that perhaps some of the differences between interpretations are influenced by viewing opposite abuses of scriptural teaching. On the one hand there are 'men who are keeping women down unbiblically and unjustly'. On the other there are 'strident, assertive "I must be free to develop myself" women'. Both need to look afresh at what the Bible teaches on marriage and the home. Hopefully, the first part of this symposium has helped us all to do that.

Turning, then, to the second area of discussion, namely that of women in the church, we are once again confronted with creation. If there is a question as to whether the Bible teaches a hierarchy in marriage, there is an even bigger question as to whether all women are expected to be subject to all men. Is there a 'creation ordinance' of women (in general) being 'helpers' to men (in general), or does creation show an equality of male/female and any hierarchy comes after the fall?

Joyce Baldwin has outlined the perfection of creation in Genesis 1 with man (male and female) being made in God's image and being given dominion within the created world. Genesis 2, she suggests, does not bear on the subject of women's ministry as the helper-counterpart relates to the marriage relationship of 'one flesh'. Only in Genesis 3 comes the hierarchical structure of male dominance and female subjection. This was the result of the fall, not an edict for all time, and Christ died to reverse the deadly effects of the fall. In Christ there is to be mutual submission.

In contrast, Jim Hurley suggests that Genesis 1 focuses on relations between rulers and realms, not on relations between men and women which is the subject of Genesis 2. Here he takes Paul's observation of Adam being first formed to indicate that Adam had the authoritative role of the 'firstborn', a theme which he follows comprehensively through the Old Testament into the eldership of the New. That position of authority is reinforced by Adam's naming his wife – 'the right to assign a name is the right to exercise authority.' He then points out that Paul lays the blame for the fall on Adam to whom God had given the commands regarding the tree in the garden. God holds Adam responsible, for he was 'priest for his family'.

In one or two key passages in the New Testament, Paul relates his statements about women to creation. Daphne Key concludes that these verses must therefore refer to all time and not just to particular situations facing the early church. 'In Genesis 2', she explains, 'we find that there was a creation order even before the man and woman cleaved to each other and became one flesh.'

She goes on to demonstrate that, nevertheless, women took a very active part both in worship and service in the early church, and all four contributors agree that women prayed, prophesied, were missionaries and were deacons. She agrees with Jim Hurley in holding that the eldership was (and is) barred to women; Howard Marshall agrees with them that there were no women elders in the New Testament churches. He adds, however, that although this was inevitable in terms of the culture of the day, it is noteworthy that there is no actual prohibition against women as elders and that women such as Priscilla were certainly not confined just to listening.

He sees the need to find the principles behind the rules of conduct in the New Testament and to apply the teaching, given in specific circumstances and a particular cultural setting, to the church of today. He and Jim Hurley give a very clear historical setting for the New Testament and agree on the way in which Jesus treated women with great respect (quite contrary to the culture of his day). They also agree in showing how Paul too had a profound respect for women, and was not ashamed to call many of them his fellow workers.

Against this background, Howard Marshall points out that we should not take a few key passages (some of which are as difficult as any in the New Testament) and base teaching on them which is at variance with the tenor of the rest of Scripture. With this, of course, all the other contributors would agree. Jim Hurley, with his detailed examination of eldership, sees consistency of Scripture leading to prohibition to women of the formal, authoritative teaching ministry. Daphne Key agrees, whereas Howard Marshall sees no differentiation between formal and informal teaching in the early church and shows how there could be cultural reasoning for Paul's prohibitions against certain areas of women's ministry. Joyce Baldwin has searched in vain for the laying down of a creation ordinance which would commit women to a supportive role for all time. All are clear that the tenor of Scripture is an important guide to their interpretation of the various passages – and yet there remain divergent views.

Are these differences insoluble? Obviously there are no glib answers and no easy solutions. There are strong convictions on both sides as views which have been unchallenged for centuries are being questioned. But amidst the differing interpretations we have seen, it does seem there is one area where there is considerable agreement on quite a wide view of the ministry of women, namely the 'mission field'. As all four contributors touch on the subject, it is an area that cannot be avoided and which may, according to Valerie Griffiths, have something to teach us. Undoubtedly God has given gifts to women in these situations and has used them for the building of his church, just as he did with Paul's fellow workers – men and women – in the first century.

Jim Hurley suggests that these fellow workers were 'persons who have shared with Paul in the hard and dangerous work of announcing God's saving message'. He goes on to discuss Junia[s] (that controversial person in Romans 16) and Andronicus. 'Romans 16:7', he concludes, 'tells us about two outstanding missionaries, one of whom may well have been a woman.' In *Man and Woman in Biblical Perspective* he adds

> I conclude that women and men who are missionaries should by all means teach the faith. Their activities in this area *need not be equivalent to adopting an elder's role* [my italics]. The end result of their work should be the establishing of a strong biblical church with its own government. With the establishment of such a church, the initial teaching role of the outside missionary, regardless of sex, changes. The local elders assume the teaching responsibility for their flocks.[1]

Joyce Baldwin, however, sees a considerable inconsistency in the general attitude to women in overseas missions, commenting that

> all the denominations have long given their blessing to women founding churches and working in leadership training, preaching and teaching, *provided the setting is another culture than their own* [my italics]. This procedure has been defended on the ground that the leader of the responsible sending body is male and so 'creation ordinance' is observed.

Is the acceptability of women's ministry in missions because it does not involve an authoritative leader's role or that women are in a team, or is it geographical? Against

---

[1] J. B. Hurley, *Man and Woman in Biblical Perspective*, p. 250.

the last of these Howard Marshall observes that 'the mission field overseas' is an 'increasingly anachronistic area'. The world-wide church is one church. Valerie Griffiths suggests that we need to recognize that God has called more women than men overseas where they can be 'fully involved in every aspect of the work except top administration. . . . It is not a matter of role or sex but of gift and calling. They work alongside men as colleagues.'

The picture is one of 'every member ministry' which Jim Packer (writing in the context of the home ministry) suggests gives the opportunity for the 'gifts of grace' to be used 'without the order of creation being violated'.[2] He goes on to say that 'every member ministry in the fellowship and a team of presbyters at the centre of the local church – is no doubt something which only a movement of God's Spirit can finally bring about'.

The discussion will certainly continue. Whether Scripture teaches that women should minister on an equality with men, or have a share in team ministry (with or without male leadership), or whether it teaches that women should find fulfilment in roles other than authoritative teaching and leadership, we all need God's Spirit to enlighten us and give us grace to listen to those who differ from us.

[2] J. I. Packer: *Thoughts on the role and function of women in the Church* (Grove Booklet on Ministry and Worship No 17, 1973), p. 26.

About the contributors

Joyce Baldwin was at one time a missionary with the Overseas Missionary Fellowship. Until recently, she was Dean of Women and lecturer in Old Testament at Trinity College, Bristol, becoming Principal in 1981. She has written three Tyndale commentaries, her latest being on Esther. Shortly before her retirement in 1982 she renewed contact with an old school friend who had been widowed some years before. They married in September 1983 and live in Bristol.

Elizabeth Catherwood read English at Oxford and has a London Diploma in Education. She is the elder daughter of Dr Martyn Lloyd-Jones and has been responsible for editing his many books. She is also at present editor of the women's imprint, Prisca Books. Her involvement with UCCF has been long-standing, both in serving on its Council, and in a regular commitment with her husband at International Student conferences. She has many speaking engagements at women's functions, and is the mother of three children.

David Field is married, with three children. He is Vice-Principal of Oak Hill College, London, and has written on human relationships and current issues for IVP. He is an ordained minister, and was for a time Secretary of the Theological Students' Fellowship.

Michael and Valerie Griffiths, holding degrees in Natural Sciences (Cantab) and Theology (Oxon) respectively, served as missionaries with the Overseas Missionary Fellowship in Japan. On Mike's appointment as General Director of the mission they moved to Singapore. During this time Mike travelled widely in South-East Asia and the Home Countries, and sometimes Valerie was able to accompany him. As well as looking after their home and four children, Valerie had a ministry to Japanese women both in Japan and in Singapore. She translated Ayako Miura's *The Wind is Howling* from Japanese. Mike is now Principal of London Bible College and author of several IVP books. Valerie lectures in Old Testament at the same college.

James B. Hurley is an American minister who studied personality psychology at Harvard, then theology at Westminster Theological Seminary, and he gained a Cambridge PhD for his research into 'Man and woman in 1 Corinthians'. Jim is married, with three children, and has written *Man and Woman in Biblical Perspective* for IVP. He is presently involved in applying scriptural principles to marriage and family therapy, which may lead to another book.

Daphne Key studied for a degree in Theology at Bristol University. She worked with the Theological Students' Fellowship of the UCCF, and during that time wrote Bible Study outlines. She is now an Anglican minister's wife, and mother of three children. Whenever possible, she accompanies her husband at student conferences and houseparties.

I. Howard Marshall has worked as a Methodist minister and is now Professor of New Testament Exegesis at the University of Aberdeen. He has edited, contributed to, or written, a number of IVP books, including his *Pocket*

Guide to Christian Beliefs and Tyndale Commentary on Acts. He is married, with four children.

Shirley Lees, the editor of this book, gained a German degree at London University before becoming a missionary in East Malaysia. There she translated the New Testament and shared with her doctor husband in a church-planting and teaching ministry. She is the mother of three children, one of whom was handicapped and died at the age of 14. Her book, *Drunk Before Dawn*, tells her story, as will the book she and her husband are presently writing for IVP. Shirley is now involved in writing, and shares with her husband in ministry to students, particularly at week-end houseparties and conferences. She serves on a number of mission councils, including that of the UCCF.

Oliver R. Barclay, the editor of the When Christians Disagree series, was formerly General Secretary of the Universities and Colleges Christian Fellowship. He has written a number of books on current issues for IVP.

Index of biblical references

To make this index as useful as possible, and to reflect the authors' use of biblical passages as accurately as possible, all verse-groupings are indexed separately: for example, Genesis 1:26–27 and Genesis 1:26–31 are not combined into a single entry. References in **bold type** are to whole chapters rather than individual verses.

Index of biblical references

Exodus
2 *30*
6:14 *53*
12:2 *53*
20:10 *103*
21:2, 16, 26–27 *103*
25 – 40 *159*
28:1–3 *123*
32 *124*
38:8 *123*

Leviticus
10:1 *124*
21ff. *123*

Numbers
1:2 *53*
3:12–13 *123*
16:3, 8–9, 11 *124*
27:1–11 *123*
28:9–10 *161*
30:3–17 *123*

Deuteronomy
15:12–18 *103*
21:15–17 *134, 166*
23:15 *103*
24:7 *103*
31:10–13 *125*

Joshua
2 *30*

Judges
4 *123*
4:4–5 *30*
4:4–6 *123*
4:5 *69*
5 *123*
10:18 *53*
13:23 *30*

Ruth
4:17 *165*

1 Samuel
1 *62*
7:12 *166*
21:1–6 *161*
25:17 *104*
25:28 *32*

2 Kings
2:19 *134*
4 *30*
11:3 *123*
22:11ff. *17*
22:14, 19–20 *123*

1 Chronicles
25:5–6 *123*

2 Chronicles
35:25 *123*

Psalms
127:3, 5 *36*
139:14 *96f.*

Proverbs
21:9 *26*
27:15 *26*
31 *16, 24, 33, 40f., 52, 69,
    109, 123, 204*

Isaiah
49:15 *34*
66:13 *34*

Ezekiel
16:25 *53*
37:25 *36*

Hosea
6:6 *161*

215

217

Index of biblical references

General index

Contributors to this book are indexed only when cited by another contributor. Details of the various author's contributions to the symposium may be found in the table of contents (pp. 9f.).

General index

General index

General index